The Machine Shed Roots

We opened the Iowa Machine Shed Restaurant in 1978 in rural Davenport, Iowa with just over 100 seats. Our location wasn't great and much of the equipment was old (but clean) and broke too often.

We were all pretty young and green. But we started with a powerful commitment; that commitment was a simple five word constitution- "Dedicated to the Iowa Farmer." That dedication meant that we worked to have a restaurant that wasn't just "farm" themed but would be something that farmers could be proud of. That meant using only the best pork and beef, real whipped cream on the pies, hearty soups, fresh baked goods made from scratch, and little things like genuine mashed potatoes and real butter. Although we still had a lot to learn, that dedication guided us through the early days. Even though money was tight, we were never tempted to take a cheaper route.

Thanks to you, folks like The Machine Shed from the start. The original Machine shed has been expanded and improved many times. And now, other Machine Sheds have sprung up in Des Moines, Iowa; Olathe, Kansas; Rockford Illinois; Pewaukee and Appleton, Wisconsin. Along the way we have been delighted to have received a bushel basketful of honors from farm groups like the Pork Producers and the Beef Industry Council. We're constantly trying to live up to those honors on the food we prepare and in the way we prepare and the way we bring it to you.

Mike Whalen

Thanks for your help

Heart of America

Restaurants & Inns™
True midwestern hospitality

Visit all of Heart of America's properties thrughout the midwest

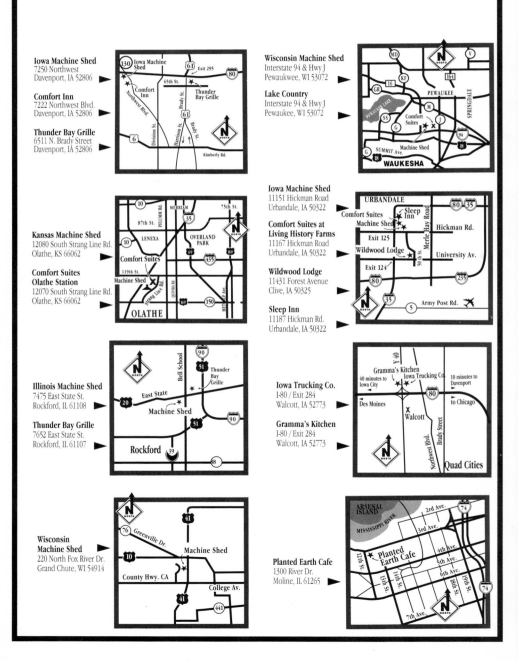

Iowa Machine Shed
7250 Northwest
Davenport, IA 52806

Comfort Inn
7222 Northwest Blvd.
Davenport, IA 52806

Thunder Bay Grille
6511 N. Brady Street
Davenport, IA 52806

Wisconsin Machine Shed
Interstate 94 & Hwy J
Pewaukwee, WI 53072

Lake Country
Interstate 94 & Hwy J
Pewaukwee, WI 53072

Kansas Machine Shed
12080 South Strang Line Rd.
Olathe, KS 66062

Comfort Suites
Olathe Station
12070 South Strang Line Rd.
Olathe, KS 66062

Iowa Machine Shed
11151 Hickman Road
Urbandale, IA 50322

Comfort Suites at
Living History Farms
11167 Hickman Road
Urbandale, IA 50322

Wildwood Lodge
11431 Forest Avenue
Clive, IA 50325

Sleep Inn
11187 Hickman Rd.
Urbandale, IA 50322

Illinois Machine Shed
7475 East State St.
Rockford, IL 61108

Thunder Bay Grille
7652 East State St.
Rockford, IL 61107

Iowa Trucking Co.
I-80 / Exit 284
Walcott, IA 52773

Gramma's Kitchen
I-80 / Exit 284
Walcott, IA 52773

Wisconsin
Machine Shed
220 North Fox River Dr.
Grand Chute, WI 54914

Planted Earth Cafe
1300 River Dr.
Moline, IL 61265

To Cookbook, Food and Farm Enthusiasts:

Meals were the fuel for the field hands of farms of the past. In this cookbook you will find the same hearty qualities of those meals.

Our "great farm fixin's" recipes were refined by **Mary Schneckloth**, a midwest food enthusiast just like you. Her passion for food creation was passed down from her mother and grandmother.

We are confident that novices as well as expert chefs will find ideas and recipes to treasure as their favorites.

Enjoy them all!

Notes & Recipes

Table of Contents

List Your Favorite Recipes

Recipes   **Page**

_____   _____

_____   _____

_____   _____

_____   _____

_____   _____

_____   _____

_____   _____

_____   _____

_____   _____

_____   _____

_____   _____

_____   _____

_____   _____

_____   _____

_____   _____

_____   _____

_____   _____

BREAKFAST

List Your Favorite Recipes

Recipes	**Page**

Applesauce-Sausage Waffles

1 lb. bulk pork sausage
1 1/2 c. all-purpose flour
4 tsp. baking powder
1 tsp. ground cinnamon
1/8 tsp. ground nutmeg

3 eggs, separated
1 1/3 c. milk
1 c. applesauce
2/3 c. vegetable oil

BROWN and crumble sausage in a skillet until no longer pink.

MEANWHILE, in a large bowl, combine flour, baking powder, cinnamon and nutmeg.

IN another bowl, beat egg yolks lightly. Add milk, applesauce and oil; mix well.

STIR into dry ingredients just until combined.

BEAT egg whites until stiff peaks form; fold into batter.

DRAIN sausage; add to batter.

BAKE in preheated waffle iron according to manufacturer's directions until golden brown.

YIELD: 8 waffles.

Baked Scrambled Eggs

2 c. soft bread cubes, crusts
 removed
1 3/4 c. milk
8 eggs, lightly beaten
3/4 tsp. salt
1/8 tsp. pepper

3 T. butter or margarine,
 divided
2 c. (8 oz.) shredded Swiss
 cheese
1/4 c. dry bread crumbs
6 bacon strips, cooked &
 crumbled

COMBINE bread cubes and milk; let stand 5 minutes.

DRAIN, reserving the excess milk.

PLACE bread in a greased 8-inch square baking dish; set aside.

COMBINE eggs and reserved milk; add salt and pepper.

MELT 2 tablespoons butter in a large skillet; add egg mixture and cook just until eggs are set.

SPOON over bread cubes.

TOP with Swiss cheese.

MELT remaining butter; add bread crumbs.

SPRINKLE over cheese.

TOP with bacon.

COVER and chill 8 hours, or overnight.

REMOVE from the refrigerator 30 minutes before baking.

BAKE, uncovered, at 325° for 35 minutes, or until heated through. Let stand 5 minutes before cutting.

YIELD: 8 servings.

Breakfast Brunch

1/2 lb. sliced bacon, diced
3/4 lb. fresh mushrooms,
   sliced
12 eggs
1 1/2 c. whipping cream
   or half & half

1/2 tsp. salt
1/8 tsp. pepper
2 c. Cheddar cheese,
   shredded
Parsley sprigs for garnish

COOK bacon until crisp. Remove from skillet with a slotted spoon; drain on paper towels. Pour off all but 2 tablespoons drippings.
ADD mushrooms and green onions in skillet; sauté over medium-low heat until liquid from mushrooms evaporates.
STIR in bacon; set aside to cool.
BEAT eggs until well mixed; add cream, salt and pepper.
STIR in cooled mushroom mixture. (Can be made ahead to this point. Refrigerate in covered container up to 24 hours.)
BUTTER an 8x12-inch shallow baking dish.
STIR 1 cup cheese into egg mixture; pour into prepared dish.
SPRINKLE remaining cheese over top.
BAKE at 325° for 35 to 40 minutes.
LET stand 5 minutes before serving. Garnish with parsley.
YIELD: 8 to 12 servings.

Breakfast Burritos

1 lb. bulk pork sausage
1 sm. onion, chopped
1/2 green pepper, chopped
1 (4 oz.) can mushroom
    stems & pieces, drained

8 flour tortillas (7"), warmed
6 eggs, beaten
1 c. shredded Cheddar
    cheese
Salsa

BROWN sausage in a skillet, drain, discarding all but 2 tablespoons drippings.
ADD onion, green pepper and mushrooms; sauté until tender.
MEANWHILE, in another skillet or in the microwave, scramble the eggs.
PLACE an equal amount of sausage mixture on each tortilla; cover with an equal amount of eggs and 2 tablespoons of cheese.
FOLD bottom of tortilla over filling and roll up. Serve with salsa, if desired.
YIELD: 4 servings.

Breakfast Fruit Bake

1 (16 oz.) can apricot
    halves, drained
1 (16 oz.) can pear halves,
    drained
1 (30 oz.) can whole plums,
    drained, halved & pitted
1 (29 oz.) can peach
    halves, drained

1 (8 oz.) can pineapple
    slices, undrained
1/3 c. packed brown sugar
1 T. butter or margarine
1/2 tsp. ground cinnamon
1/4 tsp. ground cloves

IN a greased 9x13x2-inch baking pan, starting at 9-inch end, arrange rows of fruit in the following order; half of the apricots, pears and plums, all of the peaches, then the remaining apricots, pears and plums.
DRAIN pineapple, reserving 1/2 cup of juice. Lay pineapple over fruit in pan.
IN a saucepan, combine the pineapple juice, brown sugar, butter, cinnamon and cloves. Cook and stir until sugar is dissolved and butter is melted. Pour over fruit.
BAKE, uncovered, at 350° for 20 to 25 minutes, or until heated through.
YIELD: 12 to 15 servings.

Breakfast

Breakfast Fruit Soup

6 c. water	2 1/2 c. assorted dried
4 T. quick-cooking tapioca	fruits, chopped
1 cinnamon stick (2")	1 c. pitted prunes
1 (29 oz.) can sliced	1 c. raisins
peaches with syrup	Juice of 1 lemon

IN a large heavy saucepan, bring water, tapioca and cinnamon stick to a boil; reduce heat and simmer, stirring frequently, for about 15 minutes, or until tapioca begins to thicken.

ADD remaining ingredients and continue to cook on medium heat for 15 minutes, stirring frequently.

REMOVE from heat; cover and let stand for 30 minutes. Remove cinnamon stick.

FRUIT will continue to plump up. Serve warm or cold.

YIELD: 8 to 10 servings.

Breakfast Enchiladas

1 lb. ground, fully-cooked	1 T. flour
ham	1/4 tsp. salt
1/2 c. green onions, sliced	1/4 tsp. garlic powder
1/2 c. green pepper, chopped	A few drops bottled hot
8 (7") flour tortillas	pepper sauce
4 eggs, beaten	Cheddar cheese
2 c. milk	

COMBINE ham, onion and green pepper in a bowl; place 1/3 cup of mixture and 3 tablespoons shredded Cheddar cheese in each tortilla.

ROLL up and arrange, seam-side down, on a greased 12 x 7 1/2-inch baking dish.

COMBINE eggs, milk, flour, salt, garlic powder and hot sauce. Pour over tortillas.

COVER and refrigerate several hours, or overnight.

BAKE, uncovered, in a 250° oven for 45 to 50 minutes. Sprinkle with Cheddar cheese.

BAKE a few more minutes until cheese melts. Let stand for 10 minutes.

Breakfast Nut Roll

2 c. all-purpose flour
1/2 tsp. salt
3/4 c. butter or margarine
1 (1/4 oz.) pkg. active dry
    yeast
1/2 c. + 1 tsp. sugar

1/4 c. warm water
    (110° to 115°)
2 eggs, separated
1 tsp. vanilla extract
1/2 c. chopped walnuts
Confectioners' sugar

COMBINE flour and salt; cut in butter until crumbly; set aside.

DISSOLVE yeast and 1 teaspoon sugar in warm water; let stand 10 minutes.

BEAT egg yolks; add to yeast mixture.

STIR gently into flour mixture to form a smooth ball.

DIVIDE dough in half; turn onto floured board.

ROLL each half into an 8x12-inch rectangle.

BEAT egg whites until stiff peaks form; beat in remaining sugar; fold in vanilla.

SPREAD onto each rectangle; sprinkle with nuts.

STARTING with short edge, roll up jellyroll-style, pinch ends together.

PLACE on greased baking sheet; cut a deep slit down center of each roll (do not cut through).

BAKE at once at 375° for 15 to 30 minutes, or until golden brown.

DUST with confectioners' sugar while warm. When cooled completely, slice diagonally.

YIELD: 2 rolls.

Breakfast Pizza

1 lb. pork sausage
1 pkg. (8) refrigerated
   crescent rolls
1 c. loose-packed hash
   brown potatoes, thawed
1 c. shredded sharp Cheddar
   cheese (4 oz.); may
   use Swiss or Monterey
   Jack in place of Cheddar

5 eggs
1/2 tsp. salt
2 T. grated Parmesan cheese
1/4 c. milk
1/8 tsp. pepper

IN a skillet, cook sausage until browned; drain off excess fat.

SEPARATE crescent dough into 8 triangles.

PLACE in an ungreased 12-inch pizza pie pan with points toward the center. Press over bottom and up sides to form a crust; seal perforations.

SPOON sausage over crust. Sprinkle with potatoes and top with Cheddar cheese.

IN A BOWL, beat together eggs, milk, salt and pepper. Pour into crust. Sprinkle Parmesan cheese over all.

BAKE at 375° for 25 to 30 minutes.

YIELD: 6 to 8 servings.

Breakfast Potato Pie

1 (6 oz.) pkg. hash brown
    potato mix with onions
1 qt. hot water
5 eggs
1/2 c. cottage cheese
1 c. (4 oz.) shredded
    Swiss cheese

1 green onion, chopped
1/2 tsp. salt
1/8 tsp. pepper
4 drops hot sauce
6 slices bacon, cooked &
    crumbled
Paprika

COVER hash browns with water; let stand 10 minutes. Drain well.
BEAT eggs; add potatoes and remaining ingredients except bacon
and paprika.
POUR into a well-greased 10-inch pie pan.
SPRINKLE with bacon and paprika.
COVER and refrigerate at least 8 hours.
PLACE cold pie pan, uncovered, in cold oven.
BAKE at 350° for 35 minutes, or until potatoes are tender and eggs are
done.
YIELD: 6 to 8 servings.

Breakfast Sausage Bread

2 loaves (1 lb. each) frozen
    white bread dough,
    thawed
1/2 lb. mild pork sausage
1/2 lb. hot pork sausage
1 1/2 c. diced fresh
    mushrooms
1/2 c. chopped onions

3 eggs
2 1/2 c. (10 oz.) shredded
    Mozzarella cheese
1 tsp. dried basil
1 tsp. dried parsley flakes
1 tsp. dried rosemary,
    crushed
1 tsp. garlic powder

ALLOW dough to rise until nearly doubled.

MEANWHILE, in skillet over medium heat, cook and crumble sausage. Add mushrooms and onion.

COOK and stir until sausage is browned and vegetables are tender; drain. Cool.

BEAT 1 egg; set aside.

TO sausage mixture, add 2 eggs, cheese and seasonings; mix well.

ROLL each loaf of dough into a 16x12-inch rectangle.

SPREAD half the sausage mixture on each loaf to within 1-inch of edges.

ROLL jellyroll-style, starting at a narrow end; seal edges.

PLACE on greased baking sheet.

BAKE at 350° for 25 minutes; brush with beaten egg.

BAKE 5 to 10 minutes more, or until golden brown. Serve warm.

YIELD: 2 loaves.

Breakfast Sausage Sandwiches

Softened butter or
margarine
8 slices bread
1 lb. bulk pork sausage,
cooked, crumbled &
drained

1 c. (4 oz.) shredded
Cheddar cheese
2 eggs, beaten
1 1/2 c. milk
1 1/2 tsp. prepared mustard

SPREAD butter on one side of each bread slice. Place 4 slices, buttered-side down, in a square baking dish.
TOP each bread slice with sausage and remaining bread slices, buttered-side up.
SPRINKLE with cheese.
COMBINE remaining ingredients; pour over sandwiches.
COVER and refrigerate at least 8 hours.
REMOVE from refrigerator; let stand 30 minutes.
BAKE, uncovered, at 350° for 45 minutes.
YIELD: 4 servings.

Broiled Grapefruit

3 lg. pink grapefruit
1/2 c. apricot preserves

1 T. brown sugar
1/2 c. flaked coconut

PEEL, section and seed grapefruit; place in lightly-greased individual baking dishes.
PLACE dishes on a baking sheet.
COMBINE apricot preserves and sugar in a small bowl, stirring well; spoon over grapefruit. Broil 5 1/2 inches from heat (with electric oven door partially opened) 2 to 3 minutes, or until bubbly.
SPRINKLE with coconut; broil 1 additional minute, or until coconut is lightly toasted.
YIELD: 4 servings.

Buttermilk Pancakes

1 egg	1/2 tsp. salt
1 c. all-purpose flour	1 T. sugar
1 tsp. baking powder	1 c. buttermilk
1/2 tsp. baking soda	2 T. vegetable oil

BEAT egg. Combine flour, baking powder, baking soda, salt and sugar; add to egg.

ADD buttermilk and oil, beating until mixture is smooth.

FOR each pancake, pour about 1/4 cup batter onto a hot, lightly-greased griddle.

TURN pancake when tops are covered with bubbles and edges look cooked.

SERVE warm with syrup.

YIELD: 8 pancakes.

Carol's Quiche

4 eggs	4 drops Tabasco sauce
1 1/2 c. cottage cheese	2 c. Monterey Jack cheese,
1 1/2 T. Parmesan cheese	shredded
4 T. flour	6 oz. meat (ham, crabmeat,
1 tsp. onion powder	bacon, etc.)
1/2 tsp. salt	1/2 lb. mushrooms (opt.)

BEAT eggs slightly; add remaining ingredients and mix well.

POUR into greased 10-inch pie plate.

BAKE at 350° for 45 minutes.

Cinnamon-Honey Grapefruit

1 grapefruit, halved	Dash of ground cinnamon
2 tsp. honey	

PLACE grapefruit halves, cut-side up, in an ovenproof pan.

LOOSEN grapefruit sections.

DRIZZLE each half with 1 teaspoon honey; sprinkle with cinnamon.

BROIL 2 to 3 minutes, or until bubbly.

SERVE warm.

YIELD: 2 servings.

Corned Beef Hash Eggs

3 (14 oz.) cans corned   12 eggs
  beef hash   1/2 tsp. pepper
12 (1 oz.) slices American
  cheese

SPREAD hash in the bottom of a greased 9x13x2-inch baking dish.
LAYER cheese slices over hash.
BEAT eggs and pepper; pour over top.
BAKE at 350° for 35 to 40 minutes, or until a knife inserted near the
center comes out clean.
YIELD: 8 to 10 servings.

Eggs Daffodil

15 slices bread, cubed   1 lb. Velveeta cheese
  (cut off crusts)   1 1/2 sticks butter

MELT cheese and butter; pour over bread in baking dish. Do not stir.
  8 beaten eggs   3 c. milk

MIX eggs and milk. Pour over bread. Do not stir. Refrigerate overnight. Bake 1 hour at 300°.

OPTIONAL: You can add chunked ham and/or mushrooms to eggs.

Farmer's Strata

1 lb. sliced bacon, cut
   into 1/2" pieces
2 c. chopped fully-cooked
   ham
1 sm. onion, chopped
10 slices white bread,
   cubed
1 c. cubed, cooked potatoes

2 c. (12 oz.) shredded
   Cheddar cheese
8 eggs
2 c. milk
1 T. Worcestershire sauce
1 tsp. dry mustard
Pinch of salt & pepper

IN a skillet, cook bacon until crisp; add ham and onion.
COOK and stir until onion is tender; drain.
IN a greased 9x13x2-inch baking dish; layer half the bread cubes, potatoes and cheese. Top with all of the bacon.
REPEAT layers of bread, potatoes and cheese.
IN a bowl, beat the egg; add milk, Worcestershire sauce, mustard, salt and pepper.
POUR over all. Cover and chill overnight.
REMOVE from refrigerator 30 minutes before baking.
BAKE, uncovered, at 325° for 65 to 70 minutes.
YIELD: 12 to 16 servings.

French Breakfast Puffs

1/3 c. butter or margarine, melted	1/4 tsp. ground nutmeg
	1/2 c. milk
1/2 c. sugar	1/4 c. sugar
1 lg. egg	1/2 c. ground cinnamon
1 1/2 c. all-purpose flour	2 T. butter or margarine,
1 1/2 tsp. baking powder	melted
1/2 tsp. salt	

BEAT first 3 ingredients at medium speed with an electric mixer until creamy and well blended.

COMBINE flour and next 3 ingredients; add to butter mixture alternately with milk, beginning and ending with flour mixture. Beat at low speed until blended after each addition. Spoon into greased miniature (1 3/4-inch) muffin pans, filling 2/3-full.

BAKE at 350° for 14 to 16 minutes. Remove from pans immediately.

COMBINE 1/4 cup sugar and cinnamon. Dip tops of muffins in 2 tablespoons melted butter, and then in sugar mixture.

YIELD: 28 miniature muffins.

French Toast Sandwiches

3 eggs	1 (4 oz.) ctn. whipped
1/4 c. milk	cream cheese
1 T. sugar	12 slices cinnamon bread
1 tsp. vanilla extract	

IN a bowl, beat eggs, milk, sugar and vanilla.

SPREAD 1 tablespoon cream cheese on 6 slices of bread; top with remaining slices to make 6 sandwiches.

DIP sandwiches in egg mixture.

FRY on lightly-greased skillet until golden brown on both sides.

GARNISH with fresh fruit, if desired.

YIELD: 4 to 6 servings.

Fruit Blintzes

9 eggs	1/8 tsp. salt
1 c. all-purpose flour	3 c. milk
1/4 c. cornstarch	

FILLING:	Puréed raspberries or
2 (8 oz.) pkg. cream	strawberries
cheese, softened	Whipped cream (opt.)
1/2 c. confectioners' sugar	Fresh raspberries or
	strawberries (opt.)

IN a bowl, beat eggs. Add flour, cornstarch and salt; stir until smooth.
STIR in milk. Pour 1/3 cup batter into lightly-greased 8-inch skillet.
COOK over medium heat until set and lightly browned.
TURN and cook for 1 minute. Keep in warm oven, covered with paper towels.
REPEAT with remaining batter.
FOR FILLING: Beat cream cheese and confectioners' sugar in a mixing bowl.
PLACE about 2 tablespoons in the center of each blintz; overlap sides and ends on top of filling. Place folded-side down.
TOP with puréed berries; garnish with whipped cream and fresh berries, if desired.
YIELD: 6 to 8 servings.

German Pancake

4 eggs	4 T. flour
1/2 c. milk	Pinch of salt
1 1/2 T. sugar	Sugar-cinnamon
1 tsp. baking powder	

HEAT oven to 425°.
BEAT eggs, milk, sugar, baking powder, flour and salt together.
POUR into heated oven-proof frying pan where 2 tablespoons of margarine has been melted.
BAKE for 7 minutes (pancake should not be brown).
DOT with remaining margarine, sugar and cinnamon to taste.
ROLL UP and transfer to hot platter.
YIELD: 4 servings.

Grilled Ham and Cream Cheese Breakfast Sandwiches
(Especially appealing to children)

4 slices whole wheat or
    white bread
3 oz. cream cheese

4 thin slices ham
4 T. (1/2 stick) butter

LAY 4 slices of bread on a surface and spread each side with a rounded tablespoon of cream cheese.

PLACE 2 ham slices on top of 2 of the slices and cover with the remaining bread.

MELT the butter over medium-low heat.

PLACE the sandwiches in the pan and fry gently until the bottom is golden, pressing down on each sandwich occasionally with a spatula - this will help to melt the cheese.

TURN and fry the other side.

SERVE warm.

YIELD: 2 sandwiches.

Ham and Potato Breakfast Casserole

1 (26 oz.) pkg. frozen
    shredded potatoes
1 (1 lb.) ham slice, cut
    into bite-size pieces
1 (10 3/4 oz.) can cream
    of potato soup, undiluted

1/2 tsp. pepper
1/4 c. Parmesan cheese
1 c. (4 oz.) shredded
    Cheddar cheese

COMBINE all ingredients except cheese; spoon into a lightly-greased 9x13x2-inch baking dish.

BAKE at 400° for 25 minutes; sprinkle with cheeses and bake 5 additional minutes, or until thoroughly heated.

SERVE over toasted, buttered, English muffins, or biscuits.

YIELD: 4 to 5 servings.

Honey Pancake Puff

3 T. butter or margarine
1 c. milk
6 eggs
1 (3 oz.) pkg. cream
cheese, softened

3 T. honey
1 c. all-purpose flour
1/2 tsp. salt
1/2 tsp. baking powder

PREHEAT oven to 400°.

GREASE a 12-inch, deep-dish pizza pan or iron skillet with 1 tablespoon of butter.

ADD remaining butter and place in oven until butter sizzles.

WHILE pan is in oven, place remaining ingredients in blender. Blend at high speed for 1 minute. Scrape down sides and blend at high speed 1 additional minute.

REMOVE pan from oven and immediately pour in batter.

BAKE for 20 to 25 minutes, or until puffed and dark golden brown.

REMOVE from oven and sprinkle with powdered sugar.

SERVE with strawberry jam, syrup or fresh fruit.

Italian Breakfast Casserole

4 med. red potatoes
2 T. cooking oil
8 eggs, lightly beaten
1 T. butter or margarine
1/2 lb. thinly-sliced fully-
cooked ham, diced

2 c. prepared spaghetti sauce
1/2 c. shredded Cheddar
cheese
1/2 c. shredded Mozzarella
cheese

IN A SKILLET, fry potatoes in oil until tender, about 10 to 15 minutes. Place in the bottom of 4 individual 16-ounce baking dishes.

IN the same skillet, scramble eggs in butter until set; spoon over potatoes.

TOP with ham, pour 1/2 cup spaghetti sauce into each casserole; sprinkle with cheese.

BAKE at 350° for 20 minutes, or until hot and bubbly.

YIELD: 4 servings.

Mexican Tortilla Pie

6 corn tortillas (6")	1 tsp. ground cumin
Cooking oil	2 c. shredded Cheddar
Salt	cheese
1 lb. ground beef	1 to 2 cans (4 oz. each)
1 lg. onion, chopped	chopped green chilies
1 med. green pepper, chopped	6 eggs
1 clove garlic, minced	1 1/2 c. milk
1 T. chili powder	1/2 tsp. salt
1 tsp. dried oregano	Sliced ripe olives (opt.)

CUT each tortilla into 8 wedges. Sauté a few at a time in hot oil until crisp. Drain on paper towels; sprinkle with salt.

IN a large skillet, cook ground beef, onion, green pepper and garlic until beef is browned and vegetables are tender; drain. Stir in chili powder, oregano and cumin.

IN a greased 9x13x2-inch baking dish, layer half of the tortilla wedges, half of the meat mixture and half of the cheese.

SPRINKLE chilies evenly over cheese.

TOP with remaining meat and cheese. Tuck remaining tortilla wedges, point-side up, around the edge of dish.

IN a small bowl, beat eggs, milk and salt.

POUR evenly over top.

BAKE, uncovered, at 375° for 25 to 30 minutes. Garnish with olives if desired.

YIELD: 10 to 12 servings.

Mushroom-Baked Eggs

8 eggs, hard-boiled
1 c. chopped fresh
   mushrooms
1 med. onion, finely
   chopped

1 T. parsley
1/3 c. tomato sauce
Salt & pepper, to taste
3 T. butter, melted
2 T. dry bread crumbs

HALVE the eggs lengthwise.

REMOVE the yolks and mash them with the mushrooms, onion and parsley.

ADD the tomato sauce, salt and pepper, and 1 tablespoon of the butter. Warm in saucepan for 2 minutes, stirring.

ARRANGE the egg whites in a shallow dish. Stuff them with the cooked egg yolk mixture.

SPRINKLE the tops with the bread crumbs, then with the remaining butter.

BAKE at 400° for 15 minutes, or until eggs are golden on top.

YIELD: 4 servings.

One-Skillet Breakfast

6 oz. bulk pork sausage
1 1/2 c. frozen hash
   brown potatoes
1/4 c. chopped onion
6 eggs

1/3 c. milk
2 T. minced fresh parsley
1/4 tsp. salt
1/2 c. shredded Cheddar
   cheese

IN a skillet, brown and crumble sausage until fully cooked.

REMOVE sausage, reserving drippings. In the drippings, cook potatoes and onion until potatoes are browned, stirring occasionally.

IN a bowl, beat eggs, milk, parsley and salt; pour over potato mixture.

ADD sausage; cook and stir gently over medium heat until eggs are set.

SPRINKLE with cheese.

COVER for 1 to 2 minutes, or until cheese melts.

YIELD: 4 servings.

One-Dish Egg Casserole

10 bacon strips, diced
1 c. sliced fresh mushrooms
1/2 c. sliced green onions
1/4 c. butter or margarine
1/4 c. all-purpose flour

1/4 tsp. salt
1/4 tsp. pepper
2 c. milk
1 1/2 c. (6 oz.) shredded
    Cheddar cheese

SCRAMBLED EGGS:
8 eggs
1/2 c. milk
1/2 tsp. pepper

1/4 tsp. salt
4 English muffins
2 T. minced fresh parsley

IN a skillet, cook bacon until crisp. Remove bacon and set aside; discard all but 2 tablespoons of drippings.

SAUTÉ mushrooms and onions in drippings until tender, set aside.

IN a saucepan, melt butter. Stir in flour, salt and pepper until smooth; cook until bubbly. Gradually stir in milk and cheese; cook and stir until thickened. Stir in bacon, mushrooms and onions; remove from the heat and set aside.

FOR SCRAMBLED EGGS: Beat eggs, milk, pepper and salt; pour into greased skillet.

COOK and stir gently until eggs are set. Remove and set aside.

CUT English muffin halves in half again.

PLACE in the bottom and up the sides of a greased 7x11x2-inch baking dish.

COVER with half the cheese sauce.

SPOON eggs over all; top with remaining sauce.

SPRINKLE with parsley.

BAKE, uncovered, at 325° for 20 to 25 minutes, or until bubbly.

LET STAND 5 minutes before serving.

YIELD: 4 to 6 servings.

Potato-Corn Pancakes

1 (16 oz.) pkg. frozen whole kernel corn, thawed	2 c. mashed potatoes
	1/2 c. all-purpose flour
	2 lg. eggs, beaten
1 sm. onion, finely chopped	3/4 tsp. salt
1/2 c. chopped green onion	1/2 tsp. ground pepper
2 tsp. vegetable oil	Vegetable cooking spray

COOK first 3 ingredients in hot oil in a large nonstick skillet over medium-high heat, stirring constantly, until crisp and tender. Remove from heat.

COMBINE mashed potatoes, flour and eggs, stirring well; stir in corn mixture, salt and pepper.

COAT a large skillet with cooking spray. Place skillet over medium heat until hot.

DROP mixture by rounded tablespoons into skillet; cook 3 minutes on each side, or until golden, wiping skillet as needed with paper towel.

DRAIN; serve with salsa.

YIELD: 14 (4-inch) pancakes.

Potato Pie

2 c. shredded, peeled potatoes (about 1 lb.)	1/2 c. milk
	1 c. chopped, fully-cooked ham
1 1/2 c. (6 oz.) shredded Cheddar cheese, divided	1/2 c. chopped onion
1 tsp. salt	1/2 tsp. pepper
4 eggs	

COMBINE potatoes, 1/2 cup cheese and 1/2 teaspoon salt.

PRESS into the bottom and up the sides of a greased 9-inch pie plate.

IN a bowl, beat eggs and milk. Add ham, onion, pepper and remaining cheese and salt; pour over potato crust (dish will be very full).

BAKE at 350° for 45 to 50 minutes, or until a knife comes out clean when inserted into the center. Let stand 5 minutes before cutting.

YIELD: 4 to 6 servings.

Breakfast

Quick Sausage Gravy

1 lb. bulk pork sausage   1 3/4 c. milk
2 T. all-purpose flour   6 warm biscuits, halved

IN a skillet, brown and crumble sausage until fully cooked; drain.
SPRINKLE with flour and blend.
GRADUALLY add milk, stirring constantly.
BRING to a boil; boil for 1 minute.
COOK until thickened.
SERVE over biscuits.
YIELD: 6 servings.

Quick Waffles

2 c. biscuit mix   1/2 c. vegetable oil
2 eggs, slightly beaten   7 oz. lemon-lime soda

IN mixing bowl, combine biscuit mix, eggs and oil.
ADD baking soda and mix well.
BAKE in a preheated waffle iron according to manufacturer's directions until golden brown.
YIELD: 4 to 5 waffles.

Sausage and Egg Casserole

1/2 lb. day-old Italian or   2 c. milk
    French bread, sliced   1/2 tsp. pepper
1 lb. bulk pork sausage,   8 oz. sliced Swiss cheese
    cooked & crumbled   1/4 c. chopped fresh parsley
8 eggs

LINE the bottom of a greased 9x13x2-inch baking dish with bread.
SPRINKLE with sausage.
BEAT eggs, milk and pepper; pour over sausage.
PRESS bread down with a spatula to absorb egg mixture.
TOP with cheese and parsley.
BAKE uncovered, at 350°, for 30 to 35 minutes, or until a knife inserted near the center comes out clean. Let stand 5 minutes before cutting.
YIELD: 8 servings.

Sausage Swirls

4 c. all-purpose flour
1/4 c. cornmeal
2 T. sugar
2 tsp. salt

2/3 c. vegetable oil
3/4 c. to 1 c. milk
2 lb. uncooked bulk pork
  sausage

COMBINE the flour, cornmeal, sugar, baking powder and salt.
STIR in oil until the mixture resembles coarse crumbs.
GRADUALLY stir in enough milk to form a soft dough. Turn onto a floured board; knead lightly for 30 seconds.
ROLL into 2 (10x16-inch) rectangles. Crumble uncooked sausage over dough to within 1/2-inch on all sides.
CAREFULLY roll up from 16-inch end. Wrap in foil; chill for at least 1 hour.
CUT into 1/2-inch slices; place 1-inch apart on ungreased baking sheets.
BAKE at 400° for 15 to 20 minutes, or until lightly browned.
SERVE warm or cold. Store in refrigerator.
YIELD: About 4 dozen.

Sour Cream-Ham Omelet

5 eggs, separated
1 1/2 c. chopped, cooked
  ham

1 (8 oz.) ctn. sour
  cream, divided
1/8 tsp. pepper
Vegetable cooking spray

BEAT egg whites (at room temperature) until stiff, but not dry; set aside.
BEAT egg yolks until thick and lemon-colored; stir in ham, 1/2 cup sour cream and pepper. Fold whites into egg yolk mixture.
COAT an ovenproof 10-inch omelet pan or heavy skillet with cooking spray; heat over medium heat until hot enough to sizzle a drop of water.
POUR egg mixture into skillet, and gently smooth surface.
REDUCE heat and cook about 5 minutes, or until puffy and light brown on bottom, gently lifting omelet at edge to judge color.
BAKE in oven at 325° for 15 to 18 minutes, or until a knife inserted in center comes out clean.
TIP skillet and loosen omelet in half and place on a warm plate.
TO SERVE, slice in wedges and garnish with remaining sour cream.
YIELD: 4 to 6 servings.

Sour Cream Pancakes

3 eggs, separated
1 1/2 c. sour cream
1 tsp. baking soda
1 1/4 c. all-purpose flour
1 tsp. baking powder

1/2 tsp. salt
1 T. sugar
3 T. butter or margarine,
   softened

BEAT egg yolks. Combine sour cream and baking soda, stir into egg yolks.

COMBINE baking powder, flour, salt and sugar; stir into sour cream mixture.

ADD butter, and beat at medium speed of an electric mixer for 30 seconds.

BEAT egg whites (at room temperature) until stiff peaks form; fold egg whites into batter.

FOR each pancake, pour 1/4 cup batter onto a hot, lightly-greased griddle.

TURN pancakes when tops are covered with bubbles and edges look covered.

YIELD: 14 pancakes.

Spicy Breakfast Lasagna

3 c. cottage cheese
1/2 c. chopped fresh
   chives, or 1/4 c. dried
1/4 c. sliced green onions
1 T. butter or margarine
18 eggs
1/3 c. milk
1/2 tsp. salt
1/4 tsp. pepper
8 lasagna noodles

4 c. shredded hash browns
1 lb. bulk pork sausage,
   cooked & crumbled
8 oz. sliced Monterey Jack
   cheese with jalapeño
   peppers (pepper Jack
   cheese)
8 oz. sliced Muenster
   cheese

COMBINE cheese, cottage cheese, chives and onions; set aside. In a large skillet, melt butter.

BEAT eggs, milk, salt and pepper; pour into skillet. Cook and stir over medium heat until very loosely scrambled, about 5 minutes. REMOVE from heat; set aside.

LINE a greased 9x13x2-inch baking dish with 4 lasagna noodles. Top with 2 cups of hash browns, scrambled eggs, sausage and half of the cottage cheese mixture. Top with Muenster cheese.Repeat next layer.

COVER and chill 8 hours, or overnight.

REMOVE from the refrigerator 30 minutes before baking.

BAKE, uncovered, at 350° for 35 to 40 minutes, or until a knife inserted near the center comes out clean. Let stand 5 minutes before cutting.

YIELD: 13 to 16 servings.

Toasted Omelet

8 eggs, beaten
1 lg. onion, finely chopped
4 T. cilantro
4 green chilies, seeded
   & finely chopped

Salt, to taste
8 slices bread, with crusts
   removed
1/3 c. oil

MIX the eggs with the onion, cilantro, chilies, and salt to taste.

SOAK the bread in this mixture for about 5 minutes, until it is slightly soft.

HEAT the oil in a large skillet and fry the bread on both sides.

POUR the remaining egg mixture equally on top of the slices.

FRY the bread slices on both sides until they are golden brown.

SERVE immediately.

Waffles

2 1/4 c. all-purpose flour	2 1/2 c. milk
4 tsp. baking powder	1/4 c. vegetable oil
2 eggs, lightly beaten	

IN a bowl, combine flour and baking powder.
MIX eggs, milk and oil; stir into dry ingredients just until combined.
BAKE in a preheated waffle iron according to manufacturer's directions until golden brown.
YIELD: 8 to 10 waffles.

HONEY-APPLE TOPPING:

2 tart apples, peeled & chopped	2 T. honey
1/3 c. apple juice or cider	1/8 tsp. ground cinnamon

COMBINE all ingredients in a blender, process until smooth.
SERVE warm or cold over waffles.
YIELD: 1 1/2 cups.

Whipped Egg and Biscuits

1/2 lb. sliced bacon, cut into 1" pieces	1/2 c. buttermilk biscuit mix
1/2 c. chopped onion	1/4 tsp. salt
3 eggs	1/8 tsp. pepper
1 1/4 c. milk	1/2 c. shredded Cheddar cheese

IN A SKILLET, cook bacon, until almost crisp; add onion. Cook, stirring frequently, until bacon is crisp and onion is tender. Drain.
TRANSFER to a 1 1/2-quart casserole.
IN a mixing bowl, beat eggs, milk, biscuit mix, salt and pepper until almost smooth.
SLOWLY pour over bacon and onion.
BAKE, uncovered, at 375° for 30 minutes, or until a knife inserted near the center comes out clean.
SPRINKLE with cheese; let stand 5 minutes before cutting.
YIELD: 6 servings.

Breakfast

BREADS, ROLLS, MUFFINS AND JAMS

List Your Favorite Recipes

Recipes   **Page**

Apple Bread

1/2 c. shortening
1 c. sugar
2 eggs
2 T. sour milk or butter-
    milk
2 c. flour

1 tsp. baking soda
1/2 tsp. salt
1 c. apples, peeled,
    chopped & diced
1/2 c. nuts (opt.)
1 tsp. vanilla

CREAM sugar and shortening; add eggs and beat well.
ADD milk, flour, baking soda and salt; beat well.
ADD apples, nuts and vanilla; pour into loaf pan.
BAKE at 350° for about 1 hour, or until it tests done.

Applesauce Nut Bread

1 c. sugar
1 c. applesauce
1/3 c. oil
2 eggs
3 T. milk
2 c. flour, sifted
1 tsp. baking soda
1/2 tsp. baking powder

1/2 tsp. cinnamon
1/4 tsp. salt
1/4 tsp. nutmeg
3/4 c. pecans, chopped
1/4 c. brown sugar
1/2 tsp. cinnamon
1/4 tsp. pecans

COMBINE sugar, applesauce, oil, eggs and milk.
ADD flour, baking soda, baking powder, spices and salt.
MIX well; pour into a 9x5x3-inch pan.
TOPPING: Combine brown sugar, cinnamon and pecans.
SPRINKLE over batter.
BAKE 1 hour at 350°. Let stand 30 minutes and remove to a rack to
cool.

Apricot Nut Loaf

3/4 c. dried apricots
1/2 c. raisins
1/3 c. oil
2 1/4 c. flour
1/2 tsp. salt
1/2 c. walnuts, chopped

1 lg. orange
2/3 c. sugar
2 eggs, beaten
2 tsp. baking powder
1 tsp. baking soda

PLACE the apricots in a bowl and add lukewarm water to cover. Let stand for 30 minutes.
REMOVE orange rind and finely chop.
DRAIN the apricots and chop coarsely; place in a bowl with orange rind and raisins. Set aside.
SQUEEZE the peeled orange; measure the juice and add enough hot water to obtain 3/4 cup liquid.
POUR the orange juice mixture over the apricot mixture. Stir in the sugar, oil and eggs. Set aside.
SIFT together the flour, baking powder, salt and baking soda.
FOLD the flour mixture into the apricot mixture in three batches. Stir in the walnuts.
SPOON the batter into a greased 9x5-inch loaf pan.
BAKE at 350° for 55 to 60 minutes, or until it tests done.
LET cool for 10 minutes before transferring to a rack.
MAKES 1 loaf.

Chocolate Zucchini Bread

3 eggs
2 c. sugar
1 c. oil
1 tsp. vanilla
2 sq. semi & unsweetened
  chocolate, melted
3 c. flour

1 tsp. salt
1 tsp. cinnamon
1 tsp. baking soda
1/2 tsp. baking powder
2 c. zucchini, grated fine
1 c. nuts

MIX together eggs, sugar, oil and vanilla.
ADD melted chocolate; mix well.
ADD flour, salt, cinnamon, baking soda and baking powder.
STIR in zucchini and nuts.
PLACE in greased 8 1/2 x 4 1/2-inch pan and bake 1 hour at 350°.

Breads

Cinnamon Swirl Orange Bread

SOFTEN 1 package active dry yeast in 1/4 cup warm water.

MIX 1 cup scalded milk, 1/2 cup sugar, 1/4 cup shortening, 1 1/2 teaspoons salt, 1 tablespoon grated orange peel and 3/4 cup orange juice; cool to lukewarm.

SIFT 6 1/2 to 7 cups all-purpose flour. Stir in 2 cups flour; beat smooth. Stir in yeast and 1 slightly beaten egg; beat well. Add enough remaining flour to make a soft dough. Turn out on lightly floured surface; knead until smooth, 10 minutes. Place in greased bowl, turning dough once. Cover and let rise until double, 1 1/4 hours.

PUNCH down; divide in half. Cover; let rest 10 minutes. Roll each half in a 7x15-inch rectangle, 1/2-inch thick.

COMBINE 1/2 cup sugar and 1 tablespoon cinnamon; spread each rectangle with half the sugar mixture. Sprinkle each with 1 teaspoon water; smooth with spatula.

ROLL, seal edge and place sealed-side down in greased 8 1/2 x 4 1/2 x 2-inch loaf pan.

COVER; let rise until double, 1 hour.

BAKE at 350° for 30 minutes.

COOL. Frost with icing made of 1 cup sifted confectioners' sugar, 1 teaspoon grated orange peel and 4 teaspoons orange juice.

YIELD: 1 loaf.

Cinnamon Flop

1 c. sugar	1 c. milk
2 c. flour	Brown sugar, cinnamon &
2 tsp. baking powder	butter for top
1 T. melted butter	

SIFT together flour, sugar and baking powder. Add butter and milk and stir until well blended.

DIVIDE mixture between two 9-inch pie or cake pans, well greased.

SPRINKLE tops with flour, then brown sugar, then cinnamon. Push chunks of butter into the dough. This makes holes and later gets gooey as it bakes.

BAKE at 350° for 30 minutes.

Breads   29

Cranberry Bread

2 c. all-purpose flour	1 egg
1 c. sugar	3/4 c. orange juice
1 1/2 tsp. baking powder	1 1/2 c. light raisins
1 tsp. salt	1 1/2 c. cranberries,
1/2 tsp. baking soda	chopped
1/4 c. butter	1 tsp. orange peel, grated

SIFT flour, baking powder, salt and baking soda into large bowl; cut in butter until mixture is crumbly.

ADD egg, orange peel and orange juice all at once.

STIR just until mixture is evenly moist; fold in raisins and cranberries.

SPOON into greased 9x5x3-inch pan.

BAKE at 350° for 1 hour and 10 minutes, or until toothpick comes out clean. Remove from pan; cool.

Crunchy Apple Bread

2/3 c. shortening	1/2 tsp. baking soda
1/2 c. sugar	1/4 tsp. salt
1/2 c. brown sugar	1 c. diced peeled apple
2 eggs	3/4 c. raisins
1/4 c. orange juice	3/4 c. chopped pecans
2 c. all-purpose flour	

CREAM shortening and sugar.

ADD eggs and orange juice; beat well.

COMBINE; flour, baking soda and salt; stir into creamed mixture.

STIR in apple, raisins and pecans.

POUR into a greased 9x5x3-inch loaf pan.

BAKE at 350° for 55 to 60 minutes, or until bread tests done.

COOL in pan 10 minutes before removing to a wire rack.

YIELD: 1 loaf.

Hobo Bread

This recipe was submitted by Carol Moriarty Parman's Aunt Bernadette Rees from Fort Dodge, Iowa.

2 c. boiling water
2 c. raisins

4 tsp. baking soda

COMBINE and let stand overnight at room temperature.
NEXT MORNING:
1 1/2 c. sugar
1 tsp. cinnamon

4 T. oil

CREAM well with raisin mixture. Add 4 cups of flour, 1/2 teaspoon salt, 1/2 cup chopped nuts.
MIX well and bake at 350° for 1 hour.
YIELD: 2 loaves.

Mango Bread

2 c. flour
2 tsp. ground cinnamon
1/2 tsp. salt
1 1/2 c. sugar
1/2 c. raisins
2 c. chopped ripe mangoes
   (about 2 to 3 mangoes)

2 tsp. baking soda
1/2 c. margarine, at room temp.
3 eggs, at room temp.
1/2 c. vegetable oil
1/4 c. shredded coconut

SIFT together flour, baking soda, cinnamon and salt; set aside.
CREAM margarine until soft; beat in eggs and sugar until light and fluffy. Beat in oil.
FOLD the dry ingredients into the creamed ingredients in three batches.
FOLD in the mangoes, 1/2 cup of the coconut, and the raisins.
SPOON the batter into two 9x5-inch greased loaf pans.
SPRINKLE over each loaf the remaining coconut.
BAKE at 350° for 50 to 60 minutes, or until they test done.
LET stand for 10 minutes before transferring to a cooling rack.
YIELD: 2 loaves.

Breads

Pineapple-Banana Nut Bread

3 c. all-purpose flour
3/4 tsp. salt
1 tsp. baking soda
2 c. sugar
1 tsp. ground cinnamon
1 c. chopped walnuts

3 eggs, beaten
1 c. vegetable oil
2 c. mashed ripe bananas
1 (8 oz.) can crushed
   pineapple, drained
2 tsp. vanilla extract

COMBINE first 5 ingredients; stir in pecans.

COMBINE remaining ingredients.

ADD to flour mixture, stirring just until dry ingredients are moistened.

SPOON batter into 2 greased and floured 8 1/2 x 4 1/2 x 3-inch loaf pans.

BAKE at 350° for 1 hour and 10 minutes, or until a toothpick inserted in center comes out clean.

COOL in pans 10 minutes; remove from pans and let cool on wire racks.

YIELD: 2 loaves.

FOR CARROT NUT BREAD: Substitute 2 cups grated carrots for 2 cups mashed bananas. Bake at 350° for 1 hour, or until a toothpick comes out clean.

FOR ZUCCHINI NUT BREAD: Substitute 2 cups coarsely shredded zucchini for 2 cups mashed bananas. Bake at 350° for 1 hour and 10 minutes, or until a toothpick comes out clean.

Raisin Bread

1 (15 oz.) box raisins	1/2 c. sugar
2 T. dry yeast	1 T. cinnamon
1 c. warm water	1 T. salt
2 c. warm milk	2 eggs, beaten
1/2 c. oil	8 to 10 c. flour

SOAK raisins 3 to 4 hours or overnight. Drain.
DISSOLVE yeast in warm water.
COMBINE milk, oil, sugar, cinnamon, salt and eggs. Beat well. Add yeast and raisins.
GRADUALLY add flour, stirring by hand. When dough becomes too stiff to stir, finish working in flour with your hands.
PLACE dough in greased bowl. Cover and let rise in warm place about 1 hour. Punch down, knead and let rise another hour.
DIVIDE dough into 5 portions and form loaves.
PLACE in greased pans and let rise another hour.
BAKE at 300° for 50 to 60 minutes.
YIELD: 5 loaves.

Spiced Rhubarb Bread

1 1/2 c. packed brown sugar	1 1/2 c. all-purpose flour
2/3 c. vegetable oil	1 tsp. salt
1 egg	1 tsp. ground cinnamon
1 c. buttermilk	1 1/2 c. diced fresh or frozen rhubarb
1 tsp. vanilla extract	1/2 c. chopped nuts (opt.)
1 tsp. baking soda	
TOPPING:	1 T. butter or margarine, melted
1/2 c. sugar	1 tsp. ground cinnamon

BEAT brown sugar, oil and egg; add buttermilk, vanilla and baking soda; mix well.
COMBINE flour, salt and cinnamon; stir into milk mixture; fold in rhubarb and nuts.
POUR into two greased 8 1/2 x 4 1/2 x 2 1/2-inch loaf pans.
SPRINKLE topping mix over top; bake at 350° for 1 hour.

Sugar and Spice Bread

2 pkg. dry yeast	1 c. hot scalded milk
1/2 c. warm water	1 unbeaten egg
1/2 c. butter	4 to 4 1/2 c. flour
1/3 c. sugar	(approx.)
2 tsp. salt	1/2 c. Malt-O-Meal

SOFTEN yeast in water.

COMBINE butter, sugar, salt and scalded milk; cool to lukewarm.

BLEND 1 egg and yeast; add 2 cups of flour and Malt-O-Meal. Beat until smooth. Add remaining flour gradually to form a stiff dough, beating well after each addition.

COVER; let rise in warm place until doubled, about 1 1/2 hours.

DIVIDE dough into 2 balls. Roll each into 7x12-inch rectangle on lightly floured board.

BRUSH dough with slightly beaten egg white. Sprinkle with mixture of 1/2 cup sugar and 1 tablespoon cinnamon.

ROLL short end toward you, jellyroll fashion. Seal well.

PLACE in greased pans, filling no more than half-full.

COVER; let rise in warm place until doubled, about 30 minutes.

BAKE at 375° for 35 to 40 minutes.

YIELD: 2 loaves.

Sweet Potato Bread

3 c. sugar	1 tsp. ground nutmeg
3 eggs, lightly beaten	1 tsp. ground allspice
2 c. cold mashed sweet	1 tsp. ground cinnamon
potatoes	1/2 tsp. salt
1 tsp. vanilla extract	1/2 tsp. baking soda
3 c. all-purpose flour	1 c. chopped pecans (opt.)
1 tsp. baking powder	

COMBINE flour, baking powder, nutmeg, allspice, cinnamon, salt and baking soda; stir into potato mixture.

FOLD in nuts if desired.

POUR into two 8 1/2 x 4 1/2 x 2 1/2-inch greased loaf pans.

BAKE at 350° for 1 hour, or until bread tests done.

COOL in pans 10 minutes before removing to wire rack to cool completely.

YIELD: 2 loaves.

Buttermilk Breakfast Doughnuts

1/4 c. vegetable shortening	1 tsp. baking soda
1 c. sugar + sugar for sprinkling	1/2 tsp. cinnamon
2 eggs	1/2 tsp. allspice
3/4 c. buttermilk	1/2 tsp. nutmeg
3 1/2 c. all-purpose flour	1 1/2 tsp. salt
2 tsp. baking powder	Oil, for frying

PLACE shortening and 1 cup sugar in large mixing bowl and beat to blend. Add eggs and beat well. Add the buttermilk and blend.

COMBINE flour, baking powder, baking soda, cinnamon, allspice, nutmeg and salt together; mix well. Add flour mixture to shortening mixture and beat just until mixed.

ROLL out dough on lightly floured board to 1/2-inch thick.

CUT doughnuts out with a 2 1/2 to 3-inch doughnut cutter and place on a sheet of waxed paper. Reroll the scraps and cut out more doughnuts until you run out of dough.

HEAT the oil to between 365° and 375°. Drop 3 to 4 doughnuts into the hot oil (don't crowd the pan). Fry each side about 2 minutes.

REMOVE and place on paper towels. Pat to remove any excess oil, and sprinkle sugar over doughnuts.

Cake Doughnuts

4 beaten eggs	3 tsp. baking powder
2/3 c. sugar	3/4 tsp. salt
1/3 c. milk	1 tsp. cinnamon
1/3 c. shortening, melted	1/2 tsp. nutmeg
3 1/2 c. sifted all-purpose flour	

BEAT eggs and sugar until light; add milk and cooled shortening.

SIFT together dry ingredients; add to first mixture and mix well. Chill dough thoroughly.

ROLL on lightly floured surface to 3/8-inch thick. Cut with floured cutter. Let stand 15 minutes.

FRY in oil heated to 375° until brown, turning once.

DRAIN on paper towel; while warm, shake in sack containing 1/2 cup sugar and 1 to 2 teaspoons cinnamon, if desired.

YIELD: 1 1/2 to 2 dozen.

Cider Doughnuts

2/3 c. packed brown
   sugar
2 eggs
1 tsp. ground nutmeg
3/4 tsp. salt
1/4 tsp. ground cinnamon
1/4 tsp. ground allspice
1/4 tsp. cardamom
6 T. butter or margarine
   melted & cooled

1 c. apple cider
3 c. all-purpose flour
1/2 c. whole wheat flour
2 tsp. baking powder
1/2 tsp. baking soda
Cooking oil for deep-
   fat frying
Confectioners' sugar (opt.)

BEAT first 7 ingredients in mixing bowl until thick, about 5 minutes. Gradually beat in butter, then cider.

COMBINE flours, baking powder and baking soda. Add to batter and beat just until blended.

COVER and refrigerate 1 hour.

DIVIDE dough in half.

TURN onto a lightly floured surface; pat to 1/2-inch thickness.

CUT with a floured 2 1/2-inch doughnut cutter. Repeat with remaining dough.

IN electric skillet or deep-fat fryer, heat oil to 375°.

FRY doughnuts, a few at a time, for 2 minutes per side.

DRAIN on paper towels. Dust with confectioners' sugar, if desired.

YIELD: about 1 1/2 dozen.

Coconut Cake Doughnuts

2 eggs	2 1/3 c. sifted all-purpose
1/2 c. sugar	flour
1/4 c. milk	2 tsp. baking powder
2 T. melted shortening or	1/2 c. flaked coconut
salad oil	

BEAT eggs with sugar until light; add milk and cooled shortening.
ADD sifted dry ingredients and coconut; stir just until blended.
CHILL mixture several hours.
ROLL on lightly floured surface to 1/2-inch thick. Cut out doughnuts
with doughnut cutter.
FRY in oil heated to 375° until brown; turn and brown on the other side
(about 1 minute per side).
DRAIN on paper towel.
SPRINKLE with sugar.
YIELD: 1 dozen doughnuts.

Filled Doughnuts

3/4 c. shortening	2 pkg. yeast
3/4 c. sugar	2 eggs, beaten
1 c. hot water	1 tsp. salt
1 c. warm water	6 or more c. flour

COMBINE shortening, sugar and warm water in large bowl; add yeast to water and set aside to dissolve.

WHEN shortening mixture has cooled, add eggs, salt, yeast mixture and flour.

TURN dough onto floured surface and knead until smooth and elastic.

COVER and set in warm place. Let rise until double.

ROLL dough about 1/2-inch thick and cut with doughnut cutter without the hole, or a drinking glass.

LET rise again until double.

FRY doughnuts in deep oil until browned, turning once.

COOL.

FILLING:

4 c. powdered sugar	2 T. flour
1 1/2 c. shortening	2 tsp. vanilla
2 egg whites	4 T. milk

COMBINE all ingredients and beat until smooth.

TO FILL DOUGHNUTS: Cut a small hole with a sharp knife; force filling into doughnut with a cookie press or cake decorator.

YIELD: 2 1/2 dozen.

VARIATION: You may want to use your favorite jelly or jam to fill your doughnuts.

YOU may also want to roll your doughnuts in granulated or powdered sugar just before they cool.

New Orleans Square Doughnuts

1 pkg. dry yeast
1/4 c. lukewarm water
3/4 c. milk, scalded
1/4 c. shortening
1/4 c. sugar

1 tsp. salt
1 egg
About 3 1/2 c. sifted
   all-purpose flour

SOFTEN yeast in lukewarm water.
COMBINE milk, shortening, sugar and salt; cool to lukewarm.
ADD 1 cup of flour; beat well. Add softened yeast and egg; mix. Add
enough of remaining flour to make soft dough. Turn out on lightly
floured surface; knead until smooth, about 8 minutes.
ROLL out dough to 10x14-inch rectangle, 1/3-inch thick.
CUT in 2-inch squares. Let rise until light, 30 to 40 minutes.
FRY in oil heated to 375° about 4 minutes, turning once.
DRAIN on paper towels. While still warm, dip in sugar.
YIELD: 3 dozen.

Potato Doughnuts

1 c. mashed potatoes
1 1/2 T. melted shortening
1/2 c. milk
1/4 c. sugar

1/2 tsp. salt
1/8 tsp. nutmeg
1 T. baking powder
2 1/2 c. flour

COMBINE mashed potatoes and shortening; add eggs and milk; beat
well.
GRADUALLY add dry ingredients and spices, mixing well.
ROLL dough 1/4 to 1/2-inch thick. Cut with doughnut cutter and fry
in hot oil until nicely browned.

Raised Doughnuts

1 pkg. active dry yeast	1 tsp. salt
1/4 c. water	1 egg
3/4 c. milk, scalded	3 1/2 to 3 3/4 c. sifted
1/4 c. shortening	all-purpose flour
1/4 c. sugar	

SOFTEN active dry yeast in warm water.

COMBINE milk, shortening, sugar and salt; cool to lukewarm.

ADD 1 cup of flour; beat well. Add softened yeast and egg; mix.

ADD enough of remaining flour to make soft dough. Turn out on lightly floured surface; knead until smooth and satiny, about 8 minutes.

PLACE in greased bowl, turning once to coat surface.

COVER and let rise until double, about 1 1/4 hours.

PUNCH down. Let rise again until double, about 55 minutes.

ROLL dough 1/3-inch thick.

CUT with floured doughnut cutter. Let rise until very light, about 30 to 40 minutes.

FRY in oil heated to 375° until browned.

DRAIN on paper towels.

WHILE warm, dip doughnuts in granulated sugar or glaze with Orange Glaze.

YIELD: 1/12 dozen.

ORANGE GLAZE: Add 1 teaspoon grated orange peel and 3 tablespoons orange juice to 2 cups sifted confectioners' sugar. Mix well.

Cream Cheese Coffee Cake

1 (3 oz.) pkg. cream
   cheese
1/2 c. margarine
1 c. sugar
2 eggs
2 c. flour

1 tsp. baking soda
1 tsp. baking powder
1/2 tsp. salt
1 tsp. vanilla
1 c. sour cream

FILLING:
1/3 c. brown sugar

1/3 c. sugar
1 tsp. cinnamon

CREAM the cream cheese, margarine and sugar. Add eggs one at a time.

SIFT dry ingredients and add alternately with the sour cream and vanilla.

STIR filling ingredients together.

POUR 1/2 the batter into a 9x9x2-inch greased cake pan.

SPRINKLE with 1/2 of the filling mixture. Pour in remaining batter and top with remaining filling.

BAKE at 350° for 45 minutes.

Dutch Apple Coffee Cake

1 pkg. active dry yeast
1/4 c. water
2/3 c. milk, scalded
1/4 c. shortening
1/3 c. sugar

1/2 tsp. salt
2 1/4 c. sifted all-purpose
   flour
2 slightly beaten eggs
1/2 c. seedless raisins (opt.)

APPLE TOPPING:
2 T. melted butter
4 c. sliced, pared tart
   apples

1/3 c. sugar
1 tsp. cinnamon
1/2 tsp. nutmeg

SOFTEN active dry yeast in warm water. Combine scalded milk, shortening, sugar and salt; cool to lukewarm.

STIR in 1 cup of the flour; add softened yeast and eggs; beat well. Add raisins and remaining flour; beat thoroughly.

COVER and let rise in a warm place until almost double.

PLACE in greased 9x13-inch pan. Brush with melted butter.

ARRANGE apple slices over batter. Sprinkle with combined cinnamon, sugar and nutmeg. Let rise 30 minutes.

BAKE at 350° for 30 to 35 minutes. Serve warm.

Orange Coffee Cake

1/4 c. butter or margarine, softened	1 1/2 c. all-purpose flour
3/4 c. sugar	2 tsp. baking powder
2 eggs	1/4 tsp. salt
1 T. orange juice	1/2 c. milk

TOPPING:

1/2 c. sugar	2 T. butter or margarine, melted
1/2 tsp. ground cinnamon	

CREAM butter and sugar; beat in eggs, one at a time. Add orange juice and peel.

COMBINE flour, baking powder and salt; add to creamed mixture alternately with milk.

POUR into a greased 9-inch square baking pan.

FOR TOPPING, combine sugar and cinnamon; sprinkle over batter. Drizzle with butter.

BAKE at 375° for 30 minutes, or until it tests done.

YIELD: 9 servings.

QUICK TIP: To check your oven temperature, buy an oven thermometer to leave in your oven. If the thermometer reads the same as the temperature you set your oven for, you're fine. If there is a discrepancy, go with the thermometer reading. In the future, set the dial higher or lower to compensate. (If you set the dial at 350° and thermometer reads 400°, then set it at 300° to get the desired 350°.)

Overnight Raspberry Coffee Cake

2 c. all-purpose flour	1 c. buttermilk
1 c. sugar	2/3 c. butter or margarine,
1/2 c. packed brown sugar	melted
1 tsp. baking powder	2 eggs, beaten
1 tsp. baking soda	1 c. fresh or frozen
1 tsp. ground cinnamon	raspberries
1/2 tsp. salt	

TOPPING:	1/2 c. chopped nuts
1/2 c. packed brown sugar	1 tsp. ground cinnamon

COMBINE flour, sugars, baking powder, baking soda, cinnamon and salt.
COMBINE in separate bowl, buttermilk, butter and eggs; add to dry ingredients and mix until well blended. Fold in berries.
POUR into a greased 9x13x2-inch baking pan.
COMBINE topping ingredients; sprinkle over batter.
COVER and refrigerate several hours or overnight.
UNCOVER and bake at 350° for 45 to 50 minutes, or until cake tests done.
YIELD: 12 to 16 servings.

Sour Cream Coffee Cake

1 c. butter	1/2 tsp. vanilla
2 c. sugar	2 c. flour, sifted
1 c. sour cream	1 tsp. baking powder
2 eggs	1/4 tsp. salt

SOFTEN butter; mix with sugar and eggs, then add sour cream and vanilla.
COMBINE flour, baking powder and salt; mix well together.
ADD to butter and sugar mixture; mix well.
POUR 1/2 the batter into a greased and floured bundt pan.

TOPPING:	1/2 tsp. cinnamon
1/2 c. chopped nuts	2 tsp. brown sugar

COMBINE topping and sprinkle 1/2 over batter in pan, then spoon remainder of batter, then remainder of topping.
BAKE at 350° for 55 to 60 minutes. Cool 1 hour, then sprinkle with powdered sugar.

Coffee Cakes and Rolls

Banana Fritters

2 eggs	1 tsp. salt
1/2 c. milk	4 lg. firm bananas
1 tsp. vegetable oil	Cooking oil for deep-
1 c. all-purpose flour	fat frying
1 tsp. baking powder	Confectioners' sugar (opt.)

BEAT eggs, milk and oil.
COMBINE flour, baking powder and salt; stir into egg mixture until smooth.
CUT bananas into quarters (about 2 inches long).
DIP each banana piece into batter to coat.
FRY banana pieces in an electric skillet or deep-fat fryer; heat oil to 375°. You may fry 2 to 3 pieces at a time until golden brown.
DRAIN on paper towels; dust with confectioners' sugar, if desired.
YIELD: 6 to 8 servings.

Best Breakfast Rolls

1 pkg. dry yeast	1/4 c. sugar
1 tsp. salt	1/2 c. dairy sour cream
2 eggs	1/2 c. melted butter

SOFTEN package of dry yeast in 1/4 cup warm water; add to above ingredients.
GRADUALLY add 2 3/4 to 3 cups flour to form a stiff dough.
LET RISE until double in size.
ROLL dough in two 12-inch circles.
BRUSH with melted butter.
COMBINE 3/4 cup sugar and 3/4 cup coconut; sprinkle over each circle.
CUT into 12 wedges; roll up, starting with wide end.
PLACE in 3 rows in a greased 9x13-inch pan. Let rise.
BAKE at 350° for 25 to 30 minutes. Leave in pan.

TOPPING:	1/4 c. butter
3/4 c. sugar	1 tsp. vanilla
1/2 c. sour cream	2 T. orange juice

COMBINE ingredients above and boil 3 minutes; pour over rolls.

Coffee Cakes and Rolls

Grandma Herbert's Cinnamon Rolls

1/2 c. sugar
1/2 c. shortening
1 1/2 tsp. salt
1 c. milk, scalded
1 c. lukewarm water

2 pkg. dry yeast
2 eggs, beaten
1/2 tsp. nutmeg (opt.)
7 c. flour

FILLING:
1 T. melted butter
1 1/2 c. brown sugar

1 T. cinnamon
1 c. raisins (opt.)

COMBINE sugar, shortening and salt in large mixing bowl. Scald milk and pour over shortening mixture.

COMBINE yeast and warm water and set aside to dissolve.

ALLOW milk mixture to cool; add beaten eggs, dissolved yeast and nutmeg. Beat well.

GRADUALLY add flour, beating well. Turn onto floured surface and knead lightly, adding only enough flour so dough can be handled. Place in greased bowl.

COVER and let rise in warm place until double in size, about 2 hours.

DIVIDE the dough in half. Roll each piece into a rectangle about 1/4-inch thick. Brush with melted butter and sprinkle with mixture of brown sugar and cinnamon. Sprinkle with raisins. Roll up like a jellyroll and cut slices 1/2-inch thick.

PLACE slices 1 inch apart in greased baking pans.

LET rise about 1 hour.

BAKE at 375° for 20 minutes.

MAY ice with confectioners' sugar icing.

Puff Pillow Buns

SOFTEN 1 package active dry yeast in 1/4 cup warm water.

POUR 1/2 cup scalded milk over 1/3 cup butter or margarine, 1/4 cup sugar and 1 teaspoon salt; stir until butter melts.

COOL until lukewarm.

ADD 2 eggs, beaten, 1 teaspoon grated lemon peel and 1 cup sifted all-purpose flour; beat well.

STIR in the softened yeast.

ADD 2 cups sifted all-purpose flour; mix well.

COVER the bowl with a damp cloth and refrigerate at least 4 hours or overnight.

CREAM CHEESE FILLING: Blend two 3-ounce packages softened cream cheese, 1 tablespoon sugar, 1 slightly beaten egg yolk and 1/2 teaspoon vanilla.

DIVIDE dough into fourths. (Refrigerate unused portion of dough.)

ON generously floured surface, roll each portion into an 8x12-inch rectangle; with floured knife, cut in six 4-inch squares.

PLACE about 1/2 tablespoon of filling in the center of each square; bring opposite corners to the center, pinching to seal.

PLACE 2-inches apart on a greased baking sheet.

BRUSH with 1 slightly beaten egg white.

LET RISE, uncovered, in a warm place until half again as large (not double), about 20 to 30 minutes.

BAKE in 400° oven 10 to 12 minutes.

SERVE warm.

YIELD: 2 dozen.

Refrigerator Rolls

From Marion Eisele of Olathe, Kansas. This recipe is over 100 years old.

2 packages yeast	2 c. boiling water
1/4 c. lukewarm water	1/2 c. sugar
2 eggs	2 tsp. salt
About 7 c. flour	3 T. shortening

COMBINE yeast into lukewarm water; pour boiling water over sugar, salt and shortening. Let cool until lukewarm and then add yeast, beaten eggs and about 4 cups of flour.

BEAT thoroughly and then add 3 more cups of flour and knead until flour is worked into the dough.

PLACE in a greased mixing bowl, cover well with waxed paper and place in refrigerator until dough rises to top of bowl. Punch down and then put in warm place to double in bulk, about 1 1/2 hours.

AFTER bread is risen, make into rolls.

BAKE in greased pan at 425° for 12 minutes.

Sticky Buns

Wish List

Sticky Buns

2/3 c. milk
1 pkg. active dry yeast
2 T. granulated sugar
3 to 3 1/4 c. flour
1 tsp. salt

1/2 c. (1 stick) cold
   butter, cut in pieces
2 eggs, lightly beaten
Grated rind of 1 lemon

TOPPING AND FILLING:

1 1/4 c. dark brown
   sugar, firmly packed
5 T. butter
1/2 c. water

3/4 c. pecans, chopped
3 T. granulated sugar
2 tsp. ground cinnamon
3/4 c. raisins

HEAT milk to lukewarm. Add the yeast and sugar and leave until frothy, about 15 minutes.

COMBINE the flour and salt in large mixing bowl; add the butter and cut in with a pastry blender until the mixture resembles coarse crumbs.

MAKE a well in the center and add the yeast mixture, eggs and lemon rind. With wooden spoon, stir from the center, incorporating flour with each turn. When it becomes too stiff, stir by hand to obtain a rough dough.

TRANSFER to a floured surface, knead until smooth; return to bowl. Cover and let rise until double in size, about 2 hours.

TOPPING: Combine brown sugar, butter and water in a heavy saucepan. Bring to a boil and boil gently until thick and syrupy, about 10 minutes.

PLACE 1 tablespoon of syrup in the bottom of each muffin cup. Sprinkle with a thin layer of chopped pecans, saving the rest for filling.

PUNCH down dough and place on a floured surface. Roll to a 12x18-inch rectangle.

FILLING: Combine granulated sugar, cinnamon, raisins and reserved nuts. Sprinkle over dough in an even layer.

ROLL up tightly from the long side, to form a cylinder; cut the cylinder into 1-inch rounds. Place each in a prepared muffin cup, cut-side up. Let rise about 30 minutes.

BAKE at 350° until golden brown, about 25 minutes.

REMOVE from the oven and invert the pans onto a sheet of waxed paper. Leave for 3 to 5 minutes, then remove buns from the pans. TRANSFER to a rack to cool. Serve sticky-side up.

THESE rolls freeze exceptionally well. Nice to have on hand for a later time.

Apple Cranberry Muffins

4 T. butter or margarine
1 egg
1/2 c. sugar
Grated rind from 1 lg.
    orange
1/2 c. fresh orange juice
1 c. flour
1 tsp. baking powder
1/2 tsp. baking soda
1 tsp. ground cinnamon

1/2 tsp. ground nutmeg
1/2 tsp. ground allspice
1/4 tsp. ground ginger
1/4 tsp. salt
1 to 2 apples
1 c. cranberries
1/2 c. walnuts, chopped
Confectioners' sugar, for
    dusting (opt.)

PREHEAT oven to 350°; grease a 12-cup muffin pan or use paper liners.

MELT the butter or margarine over gentle heat. Set aside to cool.

PLACE the eggs in a mixing bowl and whisk lightly. Add the melted butter or margarine and whisk to combine.

ADD the sugar, orange rind and juice. Whisk to blend, then set aside.

QUARTER, core and peel the apples. With a sharp knife, chop in a coarse dice to obtain 1 1/4 cups.

MAKE a well in the dry ingredients and pour in the egg mixture. With a spoon, stir until just blended.

ADD the apples, cranberries and walnuts, and stir to blend.

FILL the cups three-quarters full and bake until the tops spring back when touched lightly, 25 to 30 minutes.

TRANSFER to rack to cool. Dust with confectioners' sugar, if desired.

YIELD: 12 muffins.

Blueberry Streusel Muffins

1/4 c. butter or margarine, softened	1 1/2 c. fresh or frozen blueberries, thawed
1/3 c. sugar	1/2 c. sugar
1 egg	1/3 c. all-purpose flour
1 T. + 1 tsp. baking powder	1/2 tsp. ground cinnamon
1/2 tsp. salt	1/4 c. butter or margarine, softened
1 c. milk	
1 tsp. vanilla extract	

CREAM butter; gradually add 1/3 cup sugar, beating at medium speed of an electric mixer until light and fluffy. Add egg, beating well.

COMBINE 2 1/3 cups flour, baking powder and salt; add to creamed mixture alternately with milk, stirring well after each addition. Stir in vanilla extract and fold in blueberries.

SPOON batter into greased or paper-lined muffin pans, filling two-thirds full. Combine 1/2 cup sugar, 1/3 cup flour and cinnamon; cut in 1/4 cup butter with a pastry blender until mixture resembles crumbs. Sprinkle on top of muffin batter. Bake at 375° for 25 to 30 minutes, or until golden brown. Remove from pans immediately.

YIELD: 1 1/2 dozen.

NOTE: If using frozen blueberries, rinse and drain thawed berries; pat dry with paper towels. This will prevent discoloration of batter.

Carrot Muffins

3/4 c. margarine, at room temp.
1/2 c. dark brown sugar, firmly packed
1 egg, at room temp.
1 T. water
2 c. grated carrots

1 1/4 c. flour
1 tsp. baking powder
1/2 tsp. baking soda
1 tsp. ground cinnamon
1/4 tsp. ground nutmeg
1/2 tsp. salt

CREAM margarine and sugar until light and fluffy. Beat in egg and water.
STIR in carrots.
SIFT over the flour, baking powder, baking soda, cinnamon, nutmeg and salt. Stir to blend.
SPOON batter into prepared muffin cups, filling almost to the top.
BAKE at 350° for about 35 minutes, or until tops spring back when touched lightly.
LET stand 10 minutes before transferring to a rack.
YIELD: 12 muffins.

Cream Cheese and Bacon Muffins

1 c. whole wheat flour
1 c. all-purpose flour
1/4 c. sugar
4 tsp. baking powder
1/4 tsp. salt
1 c. milk
1/4 c. vegetable oil
2 eggs, divided

1 (8 oz.) pkg. cream cheese, softened
1/4 c. shredded Cheddar cheese
1/4 tsp. seasoned salt
4 bacon strips, cooked & crumbled

COMBINE first 5 ingredients in a large bowl.
COMBINE milk, oil and 1 egg; stir into dry ingredients just until moistened.
FILL greased or paper-lined muffin pans half-full.
BEAT creamed cheese and second egg in a mixing bowl.
ADD Cheddar cheese and seasoned salt; mix well; stir in bacon.
SPOON 2 tablespoons in the center of each muffin. Bake at 425° for 15 to 20 minutes, or until muffins test done. Serve warm.
YIELD: about 1 dozen.

English Muffins

1 pkg. active dry yeast	2 tsp. salt
1/2 c. warm water	1/4 c. shortening
1 1/2 c. milk, scalded	5 3/4 to 6 c. sifted
2 T. sugar	all-purpose flour

SOFTEN yeast in water.

COMBINE next 4 ingredients; cool to lukewarm.

STIR in 2 cups flour; beat well.

ADD enough of remaining flour to make a moderately stiff dough.

TURN OUT on a lightly floured surface; knead until smooth, 8 to 10 minutes.

PLACE in lightly greased bowl, turning dough once.

COVER; let rise until double, 1 1/4 hours.

PUNCH down; cover and let rest 10 minutes.

ROLL to slightly less than 1/2-inch on lightly floured surface.

CUT with a 3-inch round cutter. (Reroll edges.)

COVER and let rise until very light, 1 1/4 hours.

BAKE on top of range on medium-hot, greased griddle; turn frequently until done, about 30 minutes.

COOL thoroughly.

SPLIT with a fork; toast on both sides.

SERVE at once.

YIELD: 2 dozen.

These muffins are well worth the work; a pleasant change from toast. Delicious served with a variety of jellies, jams and marmalades, and, of course, always perfect as an accompaniment for tea drinkers.

Hot Buttered Rum Muffins

1/2 c. butter or margarine, softened	1/2 tsp. salt
1/2 c. sugar	1/8 tsp. ground cloves
2 lg. eggs	1/8 tsp. ground nutmeg
2 c. all-purpose flour	1/2 c. milk
2 tsp. baking powder	5 T. rum, divided
	3 T. sugar

BEAT butter at medium speed with an electric mixer until creamy. Add 1/2 cup sugar, beating well. Add eggs, one at a time, beating just until blended after each addition.

COMBINE flour and next 4 ingredients. Combine milk and 3 table-spoons rum. Add flour mixture to butter mixture, beginning and ending with flour mixture. Beat at low speed until blended, after each addition.

SPOON into greased or paper-lined muffin pans, filling three-fourths full. BAKE at 375° for 20 to 25 minutes, or until golden. Remove immediately to wire rack.

COMBINE remaining 2 tablespoons rum and 3 tablespoons sugar in a small saucepan. Cook over low heat, stirring constantly, until sugar dissolves. Brush on warm muffins.

YIELD: 1 dozen.

Home-Style Cheese Muffins

2 c. all-purpose flour	1/4 c. butter or margarine, melted
1 T. baking powder	
1/2 tsp. salt	2/3 c. shredded Cheddar cheese
1 egg, slightly beaten	
1 c. milk	

IN a bowl, combine flour, baking powder and salt.
MIX egg, milk and butter; stir in dry ingredients just until moistened.
FOLD in cheese.
FILL greased or paper-lined muffin cups two-thirds full.
BAKE at 400° for 20 to 25 minutes, or until golden brown.
YIELD: about 1 dozen.

Muffins

Icebox Bran Muffins

1 (10 oz.) box Raisin Bran   1 qt. buttermilk
5 c. flour   1 c. oil
3 c. sugar   4 beaten eggs
5 tsp. baking soda

COMBINE dry ingredients in a large bowl. Mix well.
ADD liquid ingredients. Mix well. Fill greased or paper-lined muffin pans two-thirds full.
BAKE at 400° for 15 to 20 minutes.
BAKE however many you wish for a meal; store remainder in refrigerator. Will keep about 2 weeks.

Jelly-Topped Peanut Butter Muffins

1 1/2 c. all-purpose flour   2 T. honey
2 tsp. baking powder   2 lg. eggs
1/2 tsp. salt   1 c. milk
1/2 c. cornmeal   1/4 c. grape jelly or other
3 T. sugar   flavor jelly
3/4 c. chunky peanut butter

COMBINE first 5 ingredients in a large bowl; make a well in center of mixture.
COMBINE peanut butter and honey, stirring well. Add eggs and milk, stirring until blended. Add to dry ingredients, stirring just until moistened.
SPOON batter into greaseed or paper-lined muffin pans, filling three-fourths full. Spoon 1 teaspoon jelly in center of each.
BAKE at 375° for 20 minutes or until golden. Remove from pans immediately and cool on wire racks.
SERVE warm with additional jelly, if desired.
YIELD: 1 dozen.

Oatmeal Buttermilk Muffins

1 c. rolled oats
1/2 c. butter, at room
  temp.
1/2 c. dark brown sugar,
  firmly packed
1 egg, at room temp.

1/4 c. raisins
1 c. buttermilk
1 c. flour
1 tsp. baking powder
1/2 tsp. baking soda
1/4 tsp. salt

COMBINE oats and buttermilk and let soak for 1 hour.
CREAM butter and sugar until light and fluffy; beat in egg.
SIFT flour, baking powder, baking soda and salt; stir into the butter
mixture, alternating with the oat mixture.
FOLD in the raisins (do not overmix).
FILL prepared muffin cups two-thirds full.
BAKE at 400° for 20 to 25 minutes.
YIELD: 12 muffins.

Orange Blossom Muffins

2 c. biscuit and baking
  mix
1/4 c. sugar
1 lg. egg, beaten
1/2 c. orange juice
2 T. vegetable oil

1/2 c. orange marmalade
1/2 c. chopped pecans
3 T. sugar
1 T. all-purpose flour
1/2 tsp. ground cinnamon
1/4 tsp. ground nutmeg

COMBINE biscuit mix and 1/4 cup sugar in a large bowl; make a well
in the center of mixture.
COMBINE egg, orange juice and oil; add to biscuit mixture, stirring
just until moistened. Stir in marmalade and pecans.
PLACE paper baking cups in muffin pans; spoon batter into cups,
filling two-thirds full.
COMBINE 3 tablespoons sugar and next 3 ingredients; sprinkle
evenly over batter.
BAKE at 400° for 18 minutes, or until done.
YIELD: 1 dozen.

Raisin Bran Muffins

4 T. butter or margarine	Juice of 1/2 lemon
1/2 c. whole wheat flour	2/3 c. all-purpose flour
1 1/2 tsp. ground cinnamon	1 1/2 tsp. baking soda
1/2 c. bran	1/8 tsp. salt
1/4 c. granulated sugar	1/2 c. raisins
1/3 c. brown sugar, firmly	1 c. buttermilk
packed	1 egg

PLACE butter or margarine in a saucepan and melt over gentle heat. Set aside.

IN mixing bowl, sift together the all-purpose flour, whole wheat flour, baking soda, salt and cinnamon.

ADD the bran, raisins and sugars and stir until blended.

IN another bowl, mix together the egg, buttermilk, lemon juice and melted butter.

ADD the buttermilk mixture to the dry ingredients and stir lightly and quickly just until moistened; do not mix until smooth.

SPOON batter into prepared muffin cups, filling them almost to the top.

BAKE until golden, 15 to 20 minutes.

YIELD: 15 muffins.

Raspberry-Streusel Muffins

1 3/4 c. all-purpose flour, divided
2 tsp. baking powder
1/2 c. sugar
1 lg. egg, lightly beaten
1/2 c. milk
1/2 c. butter, melted
1 c. frozen, unsweetened raspberries
2 T. butter or margarine, melted
1/4 c. chopped pecans
1/4 c. firmly packed brown sugar

COMBINE 1 1/2 cups flour, baking powder and sugar in a large bowl; make a well in center of mixture.

COMBINE egg, milk and 1/2 cup butter; add to dry ingredients, stirring just until moistened. Fold in raspberries. Spoon into greased or paper-lined muffin pans, filling two-thirds full.

COMBINE remaining 1/4 cup flour, 2 tablespoons butter, pecans and brown sugar; sprinkle over muffins.

BAKE at 375° for 20 to 25 minutes.

YIELD: 1 dozen.

Rhubarb Muffins

1 1/2 c. brown sugar
1/2 c. oil
1 egg
2 tsp. vanilla
1 c. buttermilk
2 1/2 c. flour
1 tsp. baking powder
1 tsp. baking soda
1/2 tsp. salt
1 1/2 c. rhubarb, finely chopped
1 T. margarine, melted
1/2 c. white sugar
1 tsp. cinnamon

COMBINE brown sugar and oil.

BEAT egg, vanilla and buttermilk well.

COMBINE flour, baking powder, baking soda and salt; mix all together and add chopped rhubarb and nuts.

SPOON batter into greased or paper-lined muffin pans to one-half full.

COMBINE 1 tablespoon margarine with white sugar and cinnamon. Sprinkle over batter in muffin cups.

BAKE at 400° for 20 minutes.

YIELD: about 1 dozen.

Muffins

Sour Cream Cornmeal Muffins

1 c. yellow cornmeal	3/4 tsp. salt
1 c. flour	1 egg, beaten
1/3 c. sugar	1 1/4 c. sour cream
2 tsp. baking powder	1/4 c. shortening
1 tsp. baking soda	

COMBINE first 6 ingredients.
STIR together egg, sour cream and shortening.
ADD to dry ingredients; mix well.
POUR batter into greased or paper-lined muffin pan to two-thirds full.
BAKE at 425° oven to 15 minutes.
THESE muffins keep very well; stay nice and moist.

Twin Mountain Muffins

1/4 c. butter or margarine, softened	2 c. all-purpose flour
	4 tsp. baking powder
1/4 c. sugar	1/2 tsp. salt
1 lg. egg	1 c. milk

BEAT butter and sugar at medium speed with an electric mixer until creamy; add egg, beating just until blended.
COMBINE flour, baking powder and salt; add to butter mixture alternately with milk, ending with flour mixture.
SPOON batter in greased or paper-lined muffin pans, filling two-thirds full.
BAKE at 375° for 25 minutes. Remove from pans immediately and cool on wire racks.
YIELD: 1 dozen.

VARIATIONS:
PEPPER-CHEESE MUFFINS: Reduce the sugar to 2 tablespoons; stir in 1 cup shredded Monterey Jack cheese with jalapeño peppers with the flour mixture.
BACON-CHEESE MUFFINS: Reduce sugar to 2 tablespoons; stir in 1/2 cup shredded Cheddar cheese and 3 slices bacon, cooked and crumbled, with the flour mixture.
HERB MUFFINS: Reduce sugar to 2 tablespoons; stir in 1 teaspoon instant minced onion, 2 teaspoons dried parsley flakes, 1 teaspoon dried oregano and 1/2 teaspoon pepper with the flour mixture.

Almond Syrup

2 T. butter or margarine   1 1/2 c. liquid brown
1/2 c. sliced almonds   sugar
                                                  1/2 tsp. almond extract

MELT butter in a small saucepan; add almonds and sauté over medium heat until golden.
STIR in sugar and almond extract.
SERVE warm.
YIELD: 1 2/3 cups.

SAVE leftover waffles and pancakes and use when serving creamed meat or vegetable sauces.

Freezer Strawberry Jam

3 c. crushed strawberries   1 (1 3/4 oz. pkg.)
5 c. sugar   powdered pectin
3/4 c. water

COMBINE strawberries and sugar; let stand 20 minutes, stirring constantly.
COMBINE water and pectin in a small saucepan; bring to a boil.
BOIL 1 minute, stirring constantly.
ADD to fruit and stir 3 minutes.
QUICKLY spoon into freezer containers of hot, sterilized jars, leaving 1/2-inch headspace.
COVER at once with plastic or metal lids and screw on bands.
LET stand at room temperature 24 hours; freeze.
YIELD: 7 half-pints.
NOTE: Jam may be stored in the refrigerator 3 weeks.

Homemade Maple Syrup

1 c. water   1/2 tsp. maple flavoring
2 c. sugar

BRING water to a boil in a 1-quart saucepan; add sugar and maple flavoring.
STIR to dissolve; cook 1 to 2 minutes, stirring constantly.
REMOVE from heat. Leftover syrup may be stored in the refrigerator.
YIELD: 2 cups.

Lemon-Blueberry Jam

4 c. fresh blueberries   1 (3 oz.) pkg. lemon-
2 c. sugar   flavored gelatin

IN a large saucepan, slightly crush 2 cups of blueberries.
ADD remaining blueberries and sugar; mix well.
BRING to a boil, stirring constantly.
REMOVE from heat; stir in gelatin until dissolved.
POUR hot jam into jars or containers.
COVER and cool. Refrigerate.
YIELD: 4 half-pints.

Strawberry-Rhubarb Jam

3 c. fresh or frozen
   strawberries
6 c. sugar, divided

3 c. diced, fresh or
   frozen rhubarb

IN a large saucepan, crush strawberries. Stir in 4 cups of sugar.
ADD rhubarb and lemon peel.
BRING to a full rolling boil over medium heat; boil 4 minutes.
ADD remaining sugar; return to a full rolling boil. Boil 4 minutes more.
REMOVE from the heat; skim off any foam.
POUR hot jam into hot jars, leaving 1/4-inch headspace.
ADJUST caps.
PROCESS for 10 minutes in a boiling-water bath.
YIELD: 3 pints.

SOUPS, SALADS, SANDWICHES AND SIDE DISHES

Soups, Salads, Sandwiches and Side Dishes Index

Black Bean Soup

1 to 2 c. black beans
Cooked hamburger or ham
   chunks
2 lg. onions
2 cloves garlic
2 cans chicken broth
1 to 2 whole tomatoes
2 T. sugar
1 tsp. pepper
1 T. red cooking wine
1 T. hot salsa
1 diced green pepper
2 diced onions
2 T. cilantro
1 c. elbow macaroni

SOAK beans 24 hours. Combine all ingredients; cook to a slow boil.
Lower heat and simmer 1/2 hour.

Cheddar-Ham Chowder

2 c. water
2 c. peeled, cubed
   potatoes
1/2 c. sliced carrots
1/2 c. sliced celery
1/4 c. chopped onion
1 tsp. salt
1/4 tsp. pepper
1/4 c. butter
1/4 c. all-purpose flour
2 c. milk
2 c. (8 oz.) shredded sharp
   Cheddar cheese
1 (16 oz.) can whole kernel
   corn, drained
1 1/2 c. cubed, fully-cooked
   ham

IN a large saucepan, bring the water, potatoes, carrots, celery, onion, salt and pepper to a boil.
REDUCE heat; cover and simmer for 8 to 10 minutes, or until vegetables are just tender. Remove from heat; do not drain.
MEANWHILE, in a medium saucepan, melt the butter.
BLEND in flour. Add the milk all at once; cook and stir until thickened and bubbly.
ADD cheese and stir until melted. Stir into the undrained vegetables; return large saucepan to heat. Add corn and ham; heat through.
YIELD: 6 to 8 servings.

Cheese Soup

4 chicken bouillon
   cubes
4 c. water
1 c. diced celery
1 c. diced onion

Salt & pepper, to taste
Sm. dash of curry
1 tsp. parsley flakes
1 tsp. chives

Add:

1 lb. broccoli
1 head cauliflower or
   frozen California
   Blend (1 pkg.)

2 1/2 c. diced potatoes

AFTER potatoes are well cooked,
ADD:

1 lb. Velveeta cheese,
   cubed

2 cans cream of chicken
   soup, undiluted

COOK slowly until cheese melts.
SOUP will be thick; if a thinner soup is desired, you may add skim milk until the desired consistency.

Chunky Chili

2 lg. onions, chopped
1 stalk celery, chopped
3 cloves garlic, minced
1 jalapeño pepper, finely
   chopped
1 T. vegetable oil
3 lb. boneless chuck
   roast, diced (may
   use ground beef)

2 tsp. oregano
1/2 to 1 tsp. cumin
1 (28 oz.) can whole
   tomatoes, undrained &
   chopped
1 (6 oz.) can tomato paste
1/4 c. chili powder
1/2 tsp. salt
3 1/2 c. water

SAUTÉ onion, celery, garlic and jalapeño pepper in hot oil until tender; set vegetables aside.

COMBINE meat, oregano and cumin in a Dutch oven. Cook until meat is browned; drain well.

ADD onion mixture, tomatoes, tomato paste, chili powder, salt and water to meat mixture.

BRING to a boil; reduce heat and simmer, uncovered, 1 1/2 to 2 hours, stirring occasionally.

YIELD: 5 cups.

Country Beef and Vegetable Soup

Beans will need to be soaked overnight for this soup, so you will have to plan ahead. If not enough time, see below.

1 1/2 c. dry large lima beans	1 c. frozen whole kernel corn
2 lb. beef shank cross-cuts, each 1 1/2" thick	1/4 c. chopped fresh parsley
1/8 tsp. ground cloves	1 T. vegetable oil
2 lg. celery stalks, cut into 1/2" pieces	2 med. onions, chopped
1 (13 3/4 oz.) can beef broth	3 garlic cloves, minced
2 tsp. salt	4 lg. carrots, cut into 1/2" pieces
1/2 tsp. ground black pepper	5 c. cabbage, cut into 1/2" pieces
3 med. all-purpose potatoes, cut into 3/4" pieces	1/2 tsp. ground or dried thyme leaves
	1 (14 1/2 oz.) can diced tomatoes
	1 c. frozen peas

RINSE beans with cold running water and discard any stones or shriveled beans. In a large bowl, place beans and enough water to cover by 2 inches. Cover and let stand at room temperature overnight. (Or, in a 4-quart saucepan, place beans in enough water to cover by 2 inches. Heat to boiling over high heat; cook 2 minutes. Remove from heat; cover and let stand 1 hour.) Drain and rinse beans.

IN AN 8-QUART DUTCH OVEN, heat vegetable oil over medium-high heat until hot. Add beef shanks and cook until meat is well browned on all sides. Transfer beef shanks to plate.

REDUCE heat to medium; add onions and cook, stirring occasionally, 5 minutes, or until tender. Add garlic and cloves; cook 30 seconds, stirring. Return beef shanks to Dutch oven; stir in carrots, celery, cabbage, beef broth, salt, thyme, pepper, and 4 1/2 cups of

Continued on following page.

66

Soups

Continued from preceding page.

water. Heat to boiling over high heat. Reduce heat to low; cover and simmer 1 hour, or until beef is tender.

MEANWHILE, in a 4-quart saucepan, heat beans and 5 cups of water to boiling over high heat. Reduce heat to low; cover and simmer 30 minutes, or until beans are tender. Drain beans.

WHEN BEEF IS TENDER, add potatoes and cooked beans to Dutch oven; heat to boiling over high heat. Reduce heat to low; cover and simmer 5 minutes. Stir in tomatoes and their juice; cover and simmer 10 minutes longer, or until potatoes are tender.

WITH slotted spoon, remove beef shanks from soup. Cut beef into 1/2-inch pieces; discard bones and fat. Return beef to Dutch oven (you may start by using "stew meat" from the grocers'--great time saver). Add frozen corn and peas; heat through. Sprinkle with parsley to serve.
YIELD: about 14 cups, or 8 main-dish servings.

Curried Zucchini and Corn Soup

1 lg. onion, minced	3 1/2 c. chicken stock
1 T. canola oil	2 c. whole kernel corn,
2 tsp. curry powder	drained
6 med. zucchini,	Salt & ground pepper,
trimmed & cut into	to taste
3/4" chunks	1 c. low-fat buttermilk

IN a large covered saucepan, cook onion in the oil over low heat until soft, but not browned, about 10 minutes. Add curry and cook a few minutes more, stirring.

TURN UP heat to medium and add zucchini. Stir a few minutes; add stock and bring to a boil. Simmer 20 minutes, or until zucchini is tender. ADD corn and cook 5 minutes more. Season with salt and pepper; let cool slightly.

PURÉE in a food processor or blender.

REFRIGERATE until cold.

ADD buttermilk and mix well.

SERVE lightly chilled.

YIELD: 6 servings.

Soups

Easy Chili Bean Soup

2 T. oil
1 med. onion, chopped
   fine
1 jalapeño pepper,
   seeded & chopped
   fine
4 lg. garlic cloves,
   minced
1 (14 1/2 oz.) can diced
   tomatoes

1 (10 3/4 oz.) can tomato
   purée
2 qt. chicken stock
2 (15 oz.) cans pinto
   beans, drained
1 tsp. ground cumin
1 tsp. chili powder
2 bay leaves

IN a large soup kettle or Dutch oven, heat the oil over medium heat. Add onions, jalapeño pepper and garlic; sauté until the onion softens and becomes translucent.

ADD the canned tomatoes and tomato purée. Simmer for 1 minute, then add chicken stock, canned pintos, cumin, chili powder and bay leaves.

BRING to a boil; reduce heat and simmer for 20 to 30 minutes. Remove bay leaves before serving.

YIELD: 6 servings.

Pinto Bean Soup

8 oz. pork sausage
1/2 c. chopped red
    pepper
1/2 c. chopped celery
6 c. chicken broth
1 (16 oz.) can tomatoes
1 tsp. chili powder
1/4 tsp. pepper
1 c. chopped onion

3 to 4 T. chopped jalapeño
    pepper
2 (15 oz.) cans pinto beans,
    rinsed & drained
1/2 tsp. cumin
8 oz. Cheddar cheese, cut
    into 1/2" cubes
Sour cream
Tortilla chips

COOK sausage, onion, pepper and celery in a 4-quart Dutch oven until sausage is brown and crumbly and vegetables are tender, about 10 minutes.

DRAIN off excess fat. Stir in broth, pinto beans, tomatoes plus juice, and seasonings.

BREAK tomatoes apart. Bring to a boil, stirring frequently.

LOWER heat; simmer, covered, 15 minutes.

TO SERVE, put approximately 1 ounce of cheese cubes in bottom of each soup bowl. Garnish with a dollop of sour cream and a few tortilla chips. Serve immediately.

YIELD: 10 cups.

Soups

Tortilla Soup

1 med. tomato,
   quartered
1 (14 1/2 oz.) can whole
   peeled tomatoes,
   with liquid
1 sm. onion, quartered
1 garlic clove
2 (10 1/2 oz.) cans
   condensed chicken
   broth, undiluted
1 T. minced fresh
   cilantro or parsley

1/2 tsp. chili powder
1/2 tsp. salt
1/4 tsp. pepper
1/4 tsp. ground coriander
1/4 tsp. cumin
6 (6") corn tortillas
1/4 c. cooking oil
Sour cream
Shredded Cheddar or
   Monterey Jack
   cheese

PLACE tomatoes, onion and garlic in a blender or food processor; blend until smooth. Transfer to a large saucepan.
ADD the chicken broth and seasonings; bring to a boil.
REDUCE heat and simmer for 3 minutes.
CUT tortillas into 1/4-inch strips; fry in hot oil until crisp and brown.
DRAIN. Ladle soup into bowls; top with tortilla strips, sour cream and cheese.
YIELD: 4 servings.

Vegetable Soup

1 sm. head cabbage
  (about 1 lb.), chopped
1/2 c. butter or margarine
1/2 c. all-purpose flour
1 1/2 qt. water
1 c. chopped onion
1 c. chopped carrot
1 c. chopped celery
1 (10 oz.) pkg. frozen
  mixed vegetables

1 (28 oz.) can tomatoes,
  undrained & chopped
1 (15 oz.) can tomato
  sauce with tomato bits
1 1/2 T. beef-flavored
  bouillon granules
2 lb. ground beef
1 1/2 tsp. salt
2 tsp. pepper

BROWN ground beef in a large Dutch oven, stirring to crumble.
DRAIN well, and set aside. (You may use beef stew meat instead of hamburger.)
MELT butter in same Dutch oven; add flour and cook over low heat 3 to 5 minutes, or until a smooth paste forms. Gradually add water, stirring constantly; cook over medium heat until bubbly, stirring occasionally.
ADD ground beef, or stew meat, and remaining ingredients.
BRING to a boil; reduce heat and simmer, uncovered, for 1 hour.
YIELD: 13 cups.

White Chicken Chili

1 tsp. lemon pepper
1 tsp. cumin seed
4 boneless, skinless
    chicken breast halves
1 clove garlic, chopped
    fine
1 c. chopped onion
2 (8 oz.) cans white
    corn, drained
2 (4 oz.) cans chopped
    green chilies,
    undrained

1 tsp. ground cumin
2 to 3 T. lime juice
2 (14 oz.) cans white or
    Great Northern beans,
    undrained
2/3 c. crushed tortilla
    chips
2/3 c. shredded Monterey
    Jack cheese

IN a large saucepan, combine 2 1/2 cups of water with the lemon pepper and cumin seed. Bring to a boil. Add the chicken breast halves and return to a boil. Reduce the heat to low and simmer 20 to 30 minutes, or until the chicken is fork-tender and the juices run clear.
REMOVE the chicken from the pan and cut into tiny pieces. Defat the broth; return to the saucepan. Place the chicken back in the stock.
COOK garlic in skillet with vegetable oil, 1 minute (do not burn). Add to chicken. Sauté onions in same skillet; add the onions, corn, chilies, cumin and lime juice to chicken; bring to a boil. Add beans and simmer until thoroughly heated.
SERVE in soup bowl, pouring over chips and cheese
MAKES 8 servings.

Basil and Tomato Salad

5 med. tomatoes, sliced
1/3 c. sliced, pitted ripe
   olives
1/2 c. (4 oz.) crumbled
   Feta cheese
1/2 c. olive oil
1/3 c. wine vinegar

2 T. finely-chopped basil,
   or 2 tsp. dried whole
   basil
1 clove garlic, minced
1/8 tsp. coarsely-ground
   pepper

ARRANGE tomatoes, olives and cheese in a 9x13x2-inch baking dish.
COMBINE remaining ingredients in a jar. Cover and shake vigorously. Pour dressing over tomato mixture, stirring gently. Cover and chill at least 4 hours.
YIELD: 8 servings.

Best Waldorf Salad

2 lg. tart red apples,
   unpeeled & diced
1 lg. green apple,
   unpeeled & diced
1/2 lb. seedless green
   grapes, halved

1/2 c. coarsely-chopped
   pecans
1/2 c. finely-chopped
   celery
1/3 c. raisins
1/4 c. + 2 T. mayonnaise

COMBINE all ingredients and stir well.
YIELD: 6 to 8 servings.

Broccoli Salad

3 or 4 c. chopped
  broccoli
1/2 lb. crisp bacon,
  crumbled

3/4 c. toasted sunflower
  seeds
1/2 c. sliced red onion

DRESSING:

1 c. mayonnaise
1/4 c. sugar

2 tsp. vinegar
1 tsp. Dijon mustard

MIX together and let stand a few hours before serving.

Cabbage and Fruit Salad

4 c. shredded cabbage
2 oranges, peeled &
  cut into bite-sized
  pieces
2 red apples, chopped
1 c. seedless red grape
  halves
1/4 c. raisins

1/2 c. mayonnaise or
  salad dressing
1/4 c. milk
1 T. lemon juice
1 T. sugar
1/8 tsp. salt
1/2 c. chopped pecans

IN a large bowl, toss cabbage, oranges, apples, grapes and raisins;
cover and refrigerate.
IN a small bowl, combine the mayonnaise, milk, lemon juice, sugar
and salt; cover and refrigerate.
JUST before serving, stir dressing and pecans into salad.
YIELD: 6 to 8 servings.

Cherry Tomato Salad

1 qt. cherry tomatoes, halved	1 to 2 tsp. minced fresh basil
1/4 c. vegetable oil	1 to 2 tsp. minced fresh oregano
3 T. vinegar	
1/4 c. minced fresh parsley	1/2 tsp. salt
	1/2 tsp. sugar

PLACE tomatoes in a shallow bowl. In a jar with a tight-fitting lid, combine the oil, vinegar, parsley, basil, oregano, salt and sugar; shake well. Pour over tomatoes. Cover and refrigerate overnight. Serve on lettuce bed.
YIELD: 6 to 8 servings.

Chicken Salad

3 or 4 c. cooked, diced chicken	3 eggs, hard-boiled & diced
1 1/2 c. celery, diced	2/3 c. ripe olives, sliced
1 sm. can water chestnuts, well drained & diced	1/2 c. sweet pickle relish
	1 c. mayonnaise
	Salt & white pepper, to taste
	Garlic powder, to taste

COMBINE all ingredients and mix well; serve open-faced on a leaf of lettuce over a croissant roll. Garnish with tomato slice. May add sliced grapes, pineapple, pared apples.

Submitted by Margaret A. Frick, Ankeny, IA.

Chilled Corn Salad

1 (12 oz.) can whole kernel corn, drained	2 T. cider vinegar
1 sm. onion, chopped	1 T. vegetable oil
1/2 c. chopped green pepper	1/4 tsp. salt
	1/4 tsp. pepper
	Lettuce leaves (opt.)

COMBINE all ingredients, except lettuce leaves. Cover and chill at least 4 hours. Serve on lettuce leaves, if desired.
YIELD: 4 to 6 servings.

Coleslaw

6 c. cabbage, shredded	1/2 c. milk
1 c. carrots, grated	1 c. Miracle Whip
1/4 c. sugar	1/2 c. buttermilk
1/2 tsp. salt	1/2 to 1 tsp. celery seed
1/4 tsp. pepper	3 to 4 T. onion, minced

COMBINE cabbage, carrots, sugar, salt and pepper; then mix with 1/2 cup milk and let stand in refrigerator for 20 minutes.
MIX Miracle Whip, buttermilk, celery seed and onion.
POUR over cabbage mixture and refrigerate.

Cranberry/Orange Molded Salad

1 (6 oz.) pkg. raspberry-flavored gelatin	1/4 tsp. ground cinnamon
2 c. boiling water	Dash of ground cloves
1 (16 oz.) can whole-berry cranberry sauce	2 c. diced orange sections
	Lettuce leaves (opt.)

IN a large bowl, dissolve gelatin in boiling water.
STIR in cranberry sauce, cinnamon and cloves.
CHILL until partially set.
ADD the orange sections.
POUR into an oiled 6-cup mold.
CHILL until set, about 3 hours.
UNMOLD; serve on a lettuce-lined platter, if desired.
YIELD: 8 to 10 servings.

Cucumbers in Sour Cream

3 lg. cucumbers
1 (8 oz.) ctn. sour cream
3 T. minced fresh chives
2 T. lemon juice
1/2 tsp. salt
1/4 tsp. pepper

PEEL cucumbers, if desired, and thinly slice; set aside.
COMBINE sour cream and remaining ingredients, stirring well.
STIR cucumbers into sour cream mixture; cover and chill.
YIELD: 6 servings.

Golden Fruit Cocktail

3/4 c. packed brown
  sugar
1/3 c. orange juice
1/4 c. butter or margarine
2 T. lemon juice
1 T. cornstarch
2 tsp. grated orange peel
1 c. sliced peaches
1 c. sliced pears
1 c. pineapple chunks
1 c. mandarin orange
  segments
12 maraschino cherries

IN a large saucepan, combine brown sugar, orange juice, butter, lemon juice, cornstarch and orange peel. Cook and stir until mixture boils; cook 2 more minutes. Add remaining ingredients; heat through.
YIELD: 6 to 8 servings.

Harvest Salad

1 qt. shredded lettuce
2 c. chopped apple
1 c. shredded carrots
2 bananas, sliced
1/2 c. raisins
1/2 c. Kraft coleslaw
  dressing

COMBINE ingredients in a 2-quart bowl; toss lightly. Seal and chill until serving time.
YIELD: 6 servings.

Submitted by Margaret A. Frick, Ankeny, IA.

Salads

Hot German Potato Salad

2 lb. sm. potatoes	1/2 c. vinegar
1/2 lb. bacon, cut up into	1/2 c. sugar
1" pieces	1 T. butter
1 1/2 c. water	5 T. flour

COOK potatoes until done; fry bacon. Drain, reserving 4 tablespoons in skillet. Add butter and flour. Cook gently. In small bowl, mix water, vinegar and sugar.

POUR into bacon fat and bring to boil until thickened. Pour over potatoes and bacon. Bake in 3-quart dish, covered, for 1 hour at 325°.

Layered Green Pea Salad

1 (10 oz.) pkg. frozen	1/3 c. sour cream
green peas, thawed	1 T. sugar
1/4 c. chopped onion	3/4 c. (3 oz.) shredded
1/4 c. sliced celery	Cheddar cheese
1/4 tsp. salt	6 slices bacon, cooked &
1/8 tsp. pepper	crumbled
1/8 tsp. dried basil	

LAYER first 9 ingredients, in order given, in a 1-quart serving bowl; cover and chill at least 4 hours.

TOP with bacon, and toss salad just before serving.

YIELD: 4 servings.

Mable's Ambrosia Salad

9 oranges, peeled,	1 c. honey
seeded & sectioned	1 to 2 tsp. almond extract
2 (20 oz.) cans crushed	1 c. flaked coconut
pineapple, drained	

COMBINE all ingredients; cover mixture and chill at least 8 hours.

YIELD: 8 servings.

Salads

Mandarin Orange Salad

1 (20 oz.) can pineapple chunks

1 (15 oz.) can mandarin orange segments

1 (3 oz.) pkg. tapioca pudding mix

1 (3 oz.) pkg. cook & serve vanilla pudding mix

1 (6 oz.) jar maraschino cherries, drained

2 med. firm bananas, sliced

DRAIN pineapple and oranges, reserving juices. Set fruit aside.
ADD water to juices to equal 3 cups; pour into a saucepan.
ADD pudding mixes; cook over medium-high heat, stirring constantly until thickened and bubbly, 5 to 10 minutes.
REMOVE from heat; cool.
PLACE fruit in bowl; put on dressing. Chill.
ADD bananas before serving.

Marinated Beet Salad

2 (16 oz.) cans sliced beets

1/2 c. sugar

2 tsp. dry mustard

3/4 c. cider vinegar

1 tsp. celery seeds

1/2 c. finely-chopped onions

DRAIN beets, reserving 1/2 cup juice; set aside.
COMBINE sugar and dry mustard in a small saucepan; stir well.
ADD beet juice and vinegar; bring to a boil over medium heat.
Remove from heat; stir in celery seeds.
COMBINE beets and chopped onion. Add vinegar mixture, tossing gently.
COVER and chill salad at least 8 hours.
YIELD: 8 servings.

Molded Strawberry Salad

1 (6 oz.) pkg. strawberry
    gelatin
1 1/2 c. boiling water
1 (10 oz.) pkg. frozen sweet-
    ened strawberries,
    thawed

1 (8 1/4 oz.) can crushed
    pineapple, undrained
1 c. (8 oz.) sour cream
Leaf lettuce (opt.)
Fresh strawberries (opt.)

IN a bowl, dissolve gelatin in water. Add the strawberries and pineapple.
STRAIN, reserving liquid and fruit. Set aside 1 cup of the liquid at room temperature.
POUR fruit and remaining liquid into a 5-cup mold, or 9-inch square pan, that has been coated with a nonstick cooking spray.
COVER and refrigerate until set, about 1 hour
WHISK sour cream and reserved liquid; pour over top.
COVER and refrigerate until set.
CUT into squares and place on individual plates, or unmold onto a serving platter.
GARNISH with lettuce and strawberries, if desired.
YIELD: 8 servings.

Nutty Pear Salad

3 pears, peeled, halved
    & cored
2 tsp. lemon juice
1 (3 oz.) pkg. cream
    cheese, softened
3 T. milk

1/4 tsp. dried whole
    tarragon
1/2 c. sliced celery
1/2 c. chopped dates
Lettuce leaves
1/4 c. chopped walnuts or pecans

SPRINKLE pear halves with lemon juice.
COMBINE cream cheese, milk and tarragon; beat until smooth.
STIR in celery and dates.
SPOON one-sixth of cheese mixture onto each pear half.
ARRANGE pear halves on a lettuce-lined platter; sprinkle with walnuts.
COVER and chill 1 to 2 hours.
YIELD: 6 servings.

Salads

Oriental Coleslaw

1 sm. head cabbage
8 T. green onion, chopped
2 T. butter
1 (3 oz.) pkg. slivered almonds
1 (3 oz.) pkg. sunflower seeds
1 T. sugar

1/2 c. oil
1 tsp. pepper
2 tsp. salt
2 tsp. Accent
6 T. white vinegar
1 pkg. dry Ramen noodles (broken, do not use spice packet)

MIX and set aside the cabbage and onion.
BROWN almonds and sunflower seeds in the butter.
WATCH; they burn very quickly; set aside.
MIX together sugar, oil, pepper, salt, Accent and vinegar.
TOSS cabbage with dressing and broken noodles.

Overnight Fruit Cup

1 (3 oz.) pkg. lemon-flavored gelatin
2 c. boiling water
1 (6 oz.) can frozen orange juice concentrate, thawed
1 (20 oz.) can pineapple chunks, undrained

1 (16 oz.) can sliced peaches, drained
1 (11 oz.) can mandarin orange segments, undrained
1 c. fresh strawberries
1 c. fresh blueberries
1 c. green grapes
1 firm banana, thinly sliced

IN a large bowl, dissolve gelatin in water.
ADD orange juice; mix well. Add all of the fruit; mix well. Cover and refrigerate overnight.
YIELD: 15 to 20 servings.

Pineapple and Cottage Cheese Salad

1 (3 oz.) pkg. lemon-
    flavored gelatin
1 (3 oz.) pkg. lime-
    flavored gelatin
1 c. boiling water
1 c. evaporated milk

1 (20 oz.) can crushed
    pineapple, undrained
1 c. mayonnaise
1 c. (8 oz.) cottage
    cheese
1 c. chopped nuts
1 T. horseradish sauce

IN a large bowl, dissolve the gelatin in boiling water.
COOL slightly; stir in the milk, pineapple with juice, mayonnaise,
cottage cheese, nuts and horseradish sauce. Mix well.
CHILL until partially set; pour into an oiled 8-cup mold.
CHILL for 6 hours, or overnight.
UNMOLD.
YIELD: 12 to 16 servings.

Potato Salad--Grandma's Best

7 med. potatoes
1/2 c. milk
1/3 c. sugar
1/4 c. vinegar
1 egg
4 T. butter
1 T. cornstarch
3/4 tsp. salt

3/4 tsp. celery seed
1/4 tsp. dry mustard
1/4 c. onion, chopped
1/4 c. mayonnaise or
    salad dressing
3 hard-cooked eggs,
    chopped

IN a medium saucepan, combine milk, sugar, vinegar, egg, butter,
cornstarch, salt, celery seed and dry mustard.
COOK and stir over low heat until thickened.
REMOVE from heat; blend in onions and carefully fold in dressing.
COMBINE potatoes and hard-cooked eggs; chill.
JUST before serving, sprinkle with paprika.
YIELD: 6 to 8 servings.

Southern Rice and Bean Salad

2 c. cold, cooked, long-
    grain rice
1 (16 oz.) can kidney
    beans, rinsed &
    drained
1 (8 3/4 oz.) can whole
    kernel corn, drained

1/2 c. sliced green
    onions, with tops
1/2 c. picante sauce
1/4 c. bottled Italian
    dressing
1 tsp. ground cumin

COMBINE all of the ingredients in a large salad bowl.
COVER and refrigerate until serving.
YIELD: 8 to 10 servings.

Summer Fruit Salad

1 fresh pineapple,
    peeled, cored &
    cubed
1 qt. fresh, hulled
    strawberries
1/2 c. fresh or frozen
    blueberries, thawed
1/2 c. fresh or frozen
    raspberries, thawed

1 (11 oz.) can mandarin
    oranges, drained
2 c. orange juice
1/2 c. sugar
1/4 c. sherry
1/2 tsp. almond extract
1/2 tsp. vanilla extract

COMBINE first 5 ingredients in a large bowl.
COMBINE remaining ingredients, stirring until sugar dissolves.
POUR sherry mixture over fruit mixture, tossing lightly.
COVER and chill 2 to 3 hours.
SERVE salad mixture with a slotted spoon.
YIELD: 10 servings.

12-Hour Salad

8 c. torn salad greens
1 1/2 c. chopped celery
2 med. green peppers, chopped
1 med. red onion, chopped
1 (10 oz.) pkg. frozen peas, thawed
1 c. salad dressing or mayonnaise
1 c. (8 oz.) sour cream
3 T. sugar
1 c. (4 oz.) shredded Cheddar cheese
1/2 lb. sliced bacon, cooked & crumbled

PLACE salad greens in the bottom of a 3-quart bowl or 9x13x2-inch baking dish.
TOP with layers of celery, green peppers, onion and peas; do not toss.
COMBINE salad dressing, sour cream and sugar; spread over salad.
SPRINKLE with cheese and bacon.
COVER and refrigerate overnight.
YIELD: 12 servings.

Vinaigrette Salad

2 med. carrots, cut into
    julienne strips
1/3 head cauliflower,
    cut into flowerets
1/2 bunch broccoli, cut
    into bite-size pieces

6 oz. fresh, whole green
    beans
1 head romaine or leaf
    lettuce
24 to 30 cherry tomatoes
1 (16 oz.) can diced
    beets, drained

COOK first 4 vegetables separately in boiling, lightly-salted water.
COOK carrots, cauliflower and broccoli 2 minutes. Cook green beans
5 minutes, or until crisp-tender.
IMMERSE vegetables in ice water to cool; drain and chill.
ARRANGE lettuce on individual serving plates. Arrange vegetables
separately on lettuce, and serve with Vinaigrette Dressing.
YIELD: 6 to 8 servings.

VINAIGRETTE DRESSING:
1 c. olive oil
1/4 c. wine vinegar
2 tsp. dry mustard

1/2 tsp. salt
2 shallots or scallions,
    minced

COMBINE all ingredients in a jar.
COVER tightly and shake vigorously.
YIELD: 1 1/2 cups.

Apple-Bacon-Cheese Sandwiches

2 c. shredded Cheddar
  cheese
1 med. apple, finely
  chopped
3/4 c. salad dressing or
  mayonnaise

1/2 c. finely-chopped
  walnuts
12 slices bread, toasted
  & buttered
12 bacon strips, cooked
6 hard-cooked eggs, sliced
6 tomato slices (opt.)

COMBINE cheese, apple, salad dressing and walnuts; spread on 6 slices of bread. Place 2 slices of bacon on each.
COVER with egg slices; top with tomatoes, if desired, and remaining slices of bread.
YIELD: 6 servings.

Barbecue Beef Sandwiches

1 (4 lb.) boneless chuck
  roast, trimmed
1/2 c. water
1 (14 oz.) btl. ketchup
1 (10 oz.) cola soft drink

1/4 c. Worcestershire
  sauce
2 T. prepared mustard
2 T. liquid smoke
1/4 tsp. hot sauce

COOK roast in 1/2 cup water in a 5-quart slow-cooker at high for 8 hours, or until tender.
DRAIN roast, reserving 1 cup of drippings in slow-cooker. Shred the meat, removing and discarding fat, and return to slow-cooker.
STIR in ketchup and next 5 ingredients; cook at high for 1 hour.
SERVE on buns.
YIELD: 10 cups.

Bean 'n' Burger Pockets

1 1/4 lb. ground beef
1 (14 1/2 oz.) can diced
   tomatoes, undrained
1 (8 oz.) can tomato
   sauce
1/2 c. chopped onion
1 clove garlic, minced
1 T. brown sugar
1 tsp. seasoned salt
1 tsp. chili powder
1/2 tsp. ground cumin
1/8 tsp. dried thyme
1/8 tsp. savory

1/8 tsp. marjoram
1/8 tsp. oregano
1/8 tsp. parsley flakes
1 (8 3/4 oz.) can navy
   beans, rinsed &
   drained
1 (8 3/4 oz.) can kidney
   beans, rinsed & drained
1 (8 3/4 oz.) can lima
   beans, rinsed &
   drained
5 pita breads, halved
1/2 c. shredded Cheddar
   cheese (opt.)

IN a heavy saucepan or Dutch oven, brown beef; drain. Add tomatoes, tomato sauce, onion, garlic, brown sugar and seasonings. Cover and simmer for 1 hour, stirring occasionally.
STIR in beans; heat through.
SPOON about 1/2 cup into each pita half.
TOP with cheese, if desired.
YIELD: 5 servings.

Beef and Cheese Roll-Ups

1 lb. deli roast beef,
    shaved
1 (8 oz.) pkg. spreadable
    cream cheese

4 (10") flour tortillas
1 c. carrots, shredded
1 c. Monterey Jack
    cheese, shredded
8 leaves green leaf lettuce

Spread soft cheese over 1 side of each flour tortilla. Top with shredded carrots and cheese.

LAYER lettuce and deli-style roast beef over carrots.

ROLL up tightly and wrap in plastic wrap.

REFRIGERATE 30 minutes before serving.

TO SERVE, cut each roll diagonally in half.

ROLL-UPs may be prepared ahead of time; wrap and refrigerate up to 8 hours before serving.

Chicken Salad Sandwiches

2 c. diced, cooked
    chicken
1 celery rib, diced
2 hard-cooked eggs,
    chopped
1 sm. cucumber, diced

1/3 c. salad dressing or
    mayonnaise
1/4 tsp. salt
1/8 tsp. dry mustard
1/8 tsp. white pepper
Bread or pita bread

IN a bowl, combine the first 8 ingredients. Serve on bread or in pita bread.

YIELD: 4 to 6 servings.

Chicken Taco Biscuit Wraps

1 (12 oz.) can
   refrigerated biscuits
1 c. chopped, cooked
   chicken

1 c. whole kernel corn,
   with red & green peppers
1/3 c. shredded Monterey
   Jack cheese
1/4 c. thick & chunky salsa

SEPARATE dough into 10 biscuits. Press each biscuit into a 5-inch round.
IN a small bowl, combine chicken, corn, cheese and salsa.
SPOON about 2 tablespoons mixture onto center of each round.
FOLD dough in half over filling; press edges with a fork to seal.
PLACE on ungreased cookie sheet.
BAKE at 400° for 10 to 13 minutes, or until golden brown.
YIELD: 10 wraps.

Chili Burgers

1 lb. ground beef
1 (10 3/4 oz.) can tomato
   soup, undiluted
1/2 c. chopped green
   pepper
1 T. brown sugar
1/2 tsp. salt
1/8 tsp. cayenne pepper
12 hamburger buns, split

1 (15 to 16 oz.) can
   kidney beans, rinsed &
   drained
1 c. chopped celery
1/2 c. chopped onion
1/4 c. ketchup
1 tsp. chili powder
1/2 tsp. ground mustard
1/4 tsp. pepper
1/8 tsp. garlic powder

IN a saucepan over medium heat, brown beef; drain.
ADD beans, soup, celery, green pepper, onion, ketchup, brown sugar and seasonings; bring to a boil.
REDUCE heat; cover and simmer for 30 to 40 minutes, or until vegetables are tender.
SERVE on buns.
YIELD: 12 servings.

Fish Sandwiches

1 c. mayonnaise
1/3 c. ketchup
1 tsp. dried parsley
  flakes
1 tsp. minced onion
1/2 tsp. Worcestershire
  sauce
1/4 to 1/2 tsp. hot
  pepper sauce
1/8 tsp. garlic powder
1/2 c. all-purpose flour

1/2 c. yellow cornmeal
1 tsp. salt
1/8 tsp. pepper
1/8 tsp. cayenne pepper
1 egg
1/2 c. milk
6 panfish or cod fillets,
  about 1 lb.
Cooking oil
6 hamburger buns, split
Lettuce leaves

IN a small bowl, combine the first 7 ingredients; cover and chill at least 1 hour.

IN a shallow bowl, combine the flour, cornmeal, salt, pepper and cayenne pepper.

BEAT egg and milk.

CUT fish to fit buns; dip fillets into egg mixture, then coat with flour mixture.

IN a large skillet, fry fish in a small amount of oil for 5 to 10 minutes, or until it flakes easily with a fork and is golden brown on both sides.

SERVE on buns with lettuce and sauce.

YIELD: 6 servings.

Ground Beef Calzones

1 (3.5 oz.) pkg. pepperoni
    slices
1/2 lb. lean ground beef
1 med. onion, chopped
1 clove garlic, minced
1 (6 oz.) can Italian-style
    tomato paste
1/4 c. dry red wine
1/2 tsp. salt

1/4 tsp. pepper
1/2 c. grated Parmesan
    cheese
1 c. (4 oz.) shredded
    Mozzarella cheese
1 lg. egg
1/2 c. milk
2 (10 oz.) cans refrigerated
    pizza crusts

CUT pepperoni slices in half, and set aside.

COOK ground beef, onion and garlic in a large skillet, stirring until beef crumbles; drain.

STIR in tomato paste and next 3 ingredients; cook, stirring often, 5 minutes, or until thickened. Remove from heat; stir in pepperoni and cheeses.

COMBINE egg and milk, stirring well; set aside.

UNROLL pizza crusts; cut each into 4 squares. Spoon 1/3 cup ground beef mixture onto each square, leaving a 1-inch border around edges. Brush borders lightly with egg mixture. Fold in half diagonally, and press edges together to seal. Place on lightly-greased baking sheets; brush tops of calzones with egg mixture.

BAKE at 350° for 15 minutes, or until lightly browned.

YIELD: 4 servings.

Sandwiches   **91**

Group Ham Sandwich

1 loaf French bread   Swiss cheese slices
Thinly-sliced ham

SLICE bread lengthwise.
SPREAD top of bread with mixture of:

1 tsp. poppy seeds   2 tsp. dried onions, soaked
1 T. dark or Dijon mustard   a few minutes in hot
1 T. horseradish   water
2 tsp. lemon juice   1 tsp. garlic powder or
1 stick soft margarine   garlic salt

LAYER slices of ham and Swiss cheese on bread which has been
spread with the preceding mixture. Slice loaf into small sandwiches.
Wrap loaf in tinfoil and bake at 350° for 25 minutes.

NOTE: This may be made the day before, refrigerated and baked
when needed.

Honey-Mustard Chicken Sandwiches

1/4 c. Dijon mustard   4 boneless, skinless
2 T. honey   chicken breast halves
1 tsp. dried oregano   4 sandwich buns, split
1 tsp. water   8 thin tomato slices
1/4 tsp. garlic powder   1 c. shredded lettuce
1/8 to 1/4 tsp. cayenne
   pepper

IN a bowl, combine the first 6 ingredients. Broil chicken 4 inches from
the heat for 3 minutes on each side. Brush with mustard sauce.
BROIL 4 to 6 minutes longer, or until juices run clear, basting and
turning several times.
SERVE on buns with tomato and lettuce.
YIELD: 4 servings.

Honey-Mustard Ham Biscuit Wraps

1 (12 oz.) can refrigerated   2 T. honey mustard
  buttermilk biscuits   1 T. finely-chopped red
1 c. chopped, cooked ham   onion

HEAT oven to 400°.
SEPARATE dough into 10 biscuits. Press each biscuit into a 5-inch round.
IN a small bowl, combine ham, mustard and onion.
SPOON about 2 tablespoons of mixture onto center of each biscuit.
FOLD dough in half over filling; press edges with fork to seal.
PLACE on ungreased cookie sheet.
BAKE at 400° for 10 to 13 minutes, or until golden brown.
YIELD: 10 wraps.

Hot Chicken (Field) Sandwiches

2 c. chopped chicken   Onion, to taste
2 tsp. green pepper   Celery or celery salt,
1/4 c. chopped ripe olives   to taste
2 hard-boiled eggs,   Pickles or sweet relish,
  chopped   to taste
2/3 c. American or
  Cheddar cheese,
  shredded

MIX the preceding ingredients. Moisten with salad dressing. Can be refrigerated for later use.
TO serve, butter buns and fill.
WRAP sandwiches in foil.
BAKE at 375° for 15 minutes.

Italian Beef Sandwiches

1 (3 to 4 lb.) chuck roast	1 or 2 onions
1 sm. can beef broth	Salt & pepper
1 can beer	Garlic powder
1 jar pepperoncini peppers & juice	Crushed oregano

SPRINKLE both sides of meat with spices; lay sliced onions and peppers on top of meat. Pour broth, pepper juice and beer over it.
COVER with foil and bake at 300° for 4 hours. Let cool.
SHRED meat and skim off fat, if desired. May be refrigerated until ready to serve.
HEAT and serve over rolls.
YIELD: 6 to 8 servings.

Italian Chicken-Mozzarella Melt

4 chicken breast halves, skinned & boned	4 French rolls, halved & toasted
2 T. olive oil	1 sm. zucchini, shredded
1/4 tsp. salt	1/4 c. shredded Mozzarella cheese
1/2 tsp. oregano, divided	
1 c. commercial pizza sauce	1/4 c. grated Parmesan cheese
1/2 tsp. basil	

BRUSH each piece of chicken with olive oil; sprinkle with salt and 1/4 teaspoon oregano.
COOK chicken in a grilling skillet or lightly-greased nonstick skillet over medium-high heat, about 4 minutes on each side, or until done. Set chicken aside.
COMBINE pizza sauce, basil and remaining 1/4 teaspoon oregano in a skillet; cook over medium-high heat until thoroughly heated.
REMOVE from heat; add chicken and keep warm.
PLACE rolls on a baking sheet; spread sauce evenly on bottom half of each roll. Top with chicken, zucchini and cheese.
BROIL 3 inches from heat (with electric oven door partially open), 2 to 3 minutes. Cover with tops of rolls.
YIELD: 4 servings.

Sandwiches

Ham, Cheese and Chicken Sandwich

4 skinned & boned
   chicken breast halves
1/4 tsp. seasoned salt
1/2 tsp. dried parsley
   flakes
1/2 c. teriyaki sauce

4 slices honey ham,
   folded in half
4 sandwich buns
Dijon or honey mustard
Lettuce leaves

FLATTEN each piece of chicken slightly, using a meat mallet or rolling pin.

SPRINKLE chicken with salt and parsley flakes; place in a shallow dish.

POUR teriyaki sauce over chicken, turning to coat. Cover and refrigerate for 1 hour.

DRAIN chicken. Place a folded ham slice and a folded cheese slice on each chicken breast; fold breast in half. Secure with a wooden pick.

COOK chicken, covered with grill lid, over medium-hot coals (350° to 400°) 10 to 15 minutes, or until chicken is done, turning twice.

REMOVE wooden picks, and serve chicken on buns with mustard and lettuce.

YIELD: 4 servings.

Meatball Sub Sandwich

9 submarine sandwich buns	2 T. cooking oil, divided
1 1/2 lb. lean ground beef	2 med. green peppers, julienned
1 egg	1 med. onion, sliced
1/4 c. milk	1 T. all-purpose flour
1 T. diced onion	1 (12 oz.) btl. chili sauce
1 tsp. salt	1 c. water
1/4 tsp. pepper	1 T. brown sugar
	1 tsp. ground mustard

CUT a thin slice off the top of each roll; scoop out bread from inside.
CRUMBLE 1 1/4 cups of the bread and place in a large bowl.
COVER rolls and tops with plastic wrap; set aside. To the crumbled bread, add beef, egg, milk, diced onion, salt and pepper.
SHAPE into 27 meatballs in 1 tablespoon oil for 20 to 25 minutes, or until no longer pink.
REMOVE with slotted spoon; set aside.
STIR flour into skillet. Add chili sauce and water; bring to a boil.
COOK and stir for 1 to 2 minutes. Stir in brown sugar and mustard.
Add meatballs, peppers and onion; cover and simmer for 20 minutes.
MEANWHILE, warm rolls in a 325° oven for 8 to 10 minutes.
SPOON 3 meatballs and sauce into each roll; re-place tops.
YIELD: 9 servings.

Sandwiches

Open-Faced Tuna Sandwiches

1 (6 1/8 oz.) can tuna,
    drained & flaked
1 c. chopped, unpeeled
    apple
3 T. finely-chopped
    onion
1/4 c. finely-chopped
    walnuts

1/4 c. salad dressing or
    mayonnaise
2 tsp. lemon juice
1/4 tsp. salt
1/8 tsp. pepper
4 slices bread, toasted
4 slices Monterey Jack or
    Muenster cheese

IN a bowl, combine tuna, apple, onion, walnuts, salad dressing, lemon juice, salt and pepper.
SPREAD on bread; top with a cheese slice.
BROIL 4 inches from the heat for 5 minutes, or until the cheese is melted.
YIELD: 4 servings.

Pizza Biscuit Wraps

1 (12 oz.) can refrigerated
    buttermilk biscuits
1 c. sliced, cooked
    Italian sausage

1/3 c. shredded Mozzarella
    cheese
1/3 c. chopped green bell pepper
1/3 c. pizza sauce

SEPARATE dough into 10 biscuits. Press into 5-inch rounds.
IN a small bowl, combine sausage, cheese, bell pepper and pizza sauce.
SPOON about 2 tablespoons mixture onto center of each biscuit. Fold in half over filling; press edges with fork to seal.
PLACE on ungreased cookie sheet.
BAKE at 400° for 10 to 13 minutes, or until golden brown.
YIELD: 10 wraps.

Pork Burgers

2 lb. ground pork
4 T. Open Pit barbecue
    sauce

2 T. onion flakes
1/2 tsp. Accent
1/4 tsp. salt

MIX well and broil, grill, or fry.

Sandwich For a Crowd

1/2 c. old-fashioned oats	3/4 c. warm water
1/2 c. boiling water	(110 to 115°)
2 T. butter or margarine	2 eggs, beaten
1 (16 oz.) pkg. hot roll	1 T. dried, minced onion
mix	

TOPPING:

1 egg	1 T. dried minced onion
1 tsp. garlic salt	1 T. sesame seeds

FILLING:

1/2 c. mayonnaise	1 med. green pepper,
4 tsp. prepared mustard	thinly sliced
1/2 tsp. prepared	1 med. onion, thinly
horseradish	sliced
Lettuce leaves	6 oz. thinly-sliced Swiss
8 oz. thinly-sliced, fully-	cheese
cooked ham	2 lg. tomatoes, thinly
8 oz. thinly-sliced,	sliced
cooked turkey	

IN a large bowl, combine oats, boiling water and butter. Let stand for 5 minutes. Meanwhile, dissolve yeast from hot roll mix in warm water. Add to the oat mixture with eggs and onion. Add flour mixture from hot roll mix; stir well (do not knead).

SPREAD dough into a 10-inch circle on a well-greased pizza pan.

COVER with plastic wrap coated with nonstick cooking spray. Let rise in a warm place until doubled, about 45 minutes.

BEAT egg and garlic salt; brush gently over dough. Sprinkle with onion and sesame seeds.

BAKE at 350° for 25 to 30 minutes, or until golden brown.

REMOVE from pan; cool on a wire rack. Split lengthwise.

COMBINE mayonnaise, mustard and horseradish; spread over cut-side of loaf. Layer with remaining filling ingredients.

CUT into wedges.

YIELD: 12 to 16 servings.

Sandwiches

Sausage and Cheese Spread for Hot Sandwiches

BROWN 1 (12-ounce) package ground pork sausage and 1/4 cup chopped onion in a heavy skillet; drain and return to skillet.
STIR in 1 (8-ounce) loaf process cheese spread, cubed (can use Velveeta); cook over low heat, stirring constantly, or heat in microwave until melted.
SERVE on buns immediately.
YIELD: 5 cups.

Sloppy Joe Squares

1 lb. ground beef	2 (8 oz.) pkg. refrigerated
1 (8 oz.) can tomato	crescent dinner rolls
sauce	1 c. (4 oz.) shredded
1 c. water	Cheddar cheese
1 (1 1/2 oz.) env. sloppy	1 T. milk
joe mix	1 T. sesame seeds
1 tsp. instant minced onion	

BROWN ground beef in a large skillet over medium-high heat, stirring until it crumbles. Drain and return to skillet.
STIR in tomato sauce and next 3 ingredients; bring to a boil. Reduce heat, and simmer 10 minutes.
UNROLL 1 package dinner rolls, pressing seams together; fit into bottom of lightly-greased 9x13-inch baking dish. Spread ground beef mixture over dough; sprinkle with cheese.
UNROLL remaining package of dinner rolls, pressing seams together; place over cheese. Brush dough with milk and sprinkle with sesame seeds.
BAKE at 425° for 15 minutes, or until top is golden brown.
YIELD: 6 servings.

Turkey Sub Sandwich

1 loaf French bread
1/3 c. blue cheese salad
   dressing
2 T. Dijon mustard
1 lb. smoked or cooked
   turkey, thinly sliced

12 bacon strips, cooked
   & drained
1 avocado, thinly sliced
6 tomato slices (1/4" thick)
Shredded lettuce

HALVE bread lengthwise.
SPREAD blue cheese dressing on cut-side of top of bread.
COMBINE mayonnaise and mustard; spread on cut-side of bottom of bread.
LAYER with turkey, bacon, avocado, tomato and lettuce.
COVER with top half of bread.
SLICE in desired lengths and serve.
YIELD: 6 servings.

Aunt Mary's Potato Pancakes

3 c. mashed potatoes
2 lg. eggs, lightly beaten
1 sm. onion, chopped

1/8 tsp. nutmeg
3 T. vegetable oil
Chopped fresh parsley

COMBINE first 4 ingredients and shape into 10 patties; dredge in flour.
POUR oil into a large skillet; place over medium-high heat until hot.
COOK patties, a few at a time, 3 minutes on each side, or until golden, turning once.
DRAIN on paper towels; sprinkle with parsley and serve immediately.
YIELD: 10 (4-inch) pancakes.

Baked Bean Casserole

1 lb. ground beef	1 (16 oz.) can large lima
1 c. chopped onion	or butter beans
1 (16 oz.) can red	1 c. catsup
kidney beans	1 tsp. salt
1 (16 oz.) can baby	1/2 c. brown sugar
lima beans	1/2 c. white sugar
1 (16 oz.) can pork &	2 T. vinegar
beans	3 T. yellow mustard

BROWN beef and onion; drain.
DRAIN most of liquid from all beans.
BAKE 1 hour at 350°.
YIELD: 12 to 15 servings.

Baked Cheese and Bacon Potatoes

2 lg. baking potatoes	2 T. finely-chopped
1/2 c. sour cream	green onion
1/4 c. grated Parmesan	1 tsp. prepared horseradish
cheese	Salt & pepper, to taste
4 bacon strips, cooked	4 tsp. butter or margarine
& crumbled	1/2 c. shredded sharp
	Cheddar cheese

BAKE potatoes at 425° for 45 minutes, or until tender. Remove from oven; reduce temperature to 350°.
CUT each potato in half horizontally, leaving a thin shell; carefully scoop pulp into bowl. Set potato skins aside.
TO THE PULP, add sour cream, Parmesan cheese, bacon, onion and horseradish. Mix with a fork until combined but not mashed.
ADD salt and pepper.
FILL potato skins.
TOP each potato with 1 teaspoon butter and sprinkle with cheese. Place in a shallow baking dish.
BAKE at 350° until heated through, about 20 minutes.
YIELD: 4 servings.

Baked Onion Casserole

4 med. onions, sliced	2 T. butter, melted
3 T. butter	2 oz. Swiss cheese, shredded
2 T. flour	3 T. Parmesan cheese, grated
Pepper	1/4 c. dry sherry
3/4 c. beef bouillon	1 1/2 c. plain croutons

COOK onions in butter until tender. Blend in flour and pepper; add bouillon and sherry.
COOK until bubbly and thick.
PUT into 1-quart casserole.
TOSS croutons with 2 tablespoons melted butter.
SPOON on top of onions.
SPRINKLE with cheese.
PLACE under broiler until cheese melts; 1 minute.
YIELD: 4 to 6 servings.

Buttery Macaroni-Corn Casserole

1 stick butter or margarine	1 c. Velveeta cheese, cubed
1 c. macaroni, uncooked	1 can cream-style corn
	1 can whole kernel corn

MIX all ingredients together; place in a greased 2 1/2-quart casserole.
BAKE at 350° for 45 to 60 minutes.
ESPECIALLY GOOD!

Copper Penny Carrots

This recipe was submitted by Margaret A. Frick of Ankeny, Iowa. Margaret lived in Scott, Muscatine and Cedar counties for 19 years.

2 lb. sliced carrots	1/2 c. vegetable oil
1 sm. green pepper, thinly sliced	1 c. sugar
	3/4 c. vinegar
1 med. onion, thinly sliced	1 tsp. prepared mustard
	Salt & pepper, to taste
1 (10 3/4 oz.) can tomato soup	1 tsp. Worcestershire sauce

COOK carrots in salted water until medium done; rinse in ice water.
ARRANGE layers of carrots, green pepper and onion in a bowl or container.
COMBINE remaining ingredients in saucepan and bring to a boil, stirring until thoroughly blended.
POUR marinade over vegetable layers and refrigerate until flavor is absorbed.
YIELD: 12 servings.

Hash Brown Casserole

1 pt. sour cream	2 lb. frozen hash browns, thawed
1 can cream of chicken soup	1 c. margarine, melted
3 c. Cheddar cheese, grated	2 T. minced onions
2 c. corn flakes, crushed	1 tsp. salt
	1/2 tsp. pepper

HEAT half of margarine; add to all other ingredients, except corn flakes.
MELT other half of margarine, and mix with crushed corn flakes.
PUT potatoes in a 9x12-inch pan; top with corn flakes.
BAKE at 350° for 1 hour.
YIELD: 8 to 10 servings.

Lima Bean Casserole

8 bacon strips
1 med. onion, chopped
1 (10 3/4 oz.) can
   condensed tomato
   soup, undiluted
5 slices processed
   American cheese,
   cut into 1/2" pieces

1 (16 oz.) pkg. frozen
   baby lima beans,
   cooked & drained
Additional cheese slices
   (opt.)

IN a large skillet, cook bacon until crisp. Remove to paper towel; drain, reserving 1 tablespoon of the drippings.
SAUTÉ onion in drippings until tender.
STIR in soup, cheese, beans and bacon.
COVER and simmer over low heat for 5 minutes, or until cheese melts. Spoon into ungreased 1 1/2-quart casserole.
COVER and bake at 350° for 20 to 30 minutes, or until casserole is bubbly and beans are tender.
GARNISH with additional cheese, if desired.
YIELD: 8 to 10 servings.

Mashed Potatoes

2 lb. red or Idaho
   potatoes, peeled
   & quartered

1/2 c. milk
1/4 c. butter or margarine
Salt & pepper

COVER potatoes with water in a large saucepan. Bring to boil.
REDUCE heat to medium.
COOK 20 minutes, or until tender; drain.
BEAT potatoes, milk, butter, salt and pepper with electric mixer on medium speed until fluffy, or mash until desired consistency. Serve warm.
YIELD: 4 to 6 servings.

Side Dishes

Parmesan Potatoes

6 lg. potatoes	3/4 tsp. salt
1/4 c. flour	1/8 tsp. pepper
1/4 c. Parmesan cheese	1/3 c. margarine

QUARTER potatoes.

COMBINE flour, cheese, salt and pepper in a bag.

MOISTEN potatoes with water and shake, a few at a time, in bag, coating well.

MELT margarine in a 9x13-inch baking dish.

PLACE potatoes in a layer in dish.

BAKE at 375° for 1 hour, turning once during baking.

YIELD: 6 to 8 servings.

Potato-Cheese Bake

PEEL and cook 3 to 4 pounds red or Idaho potatoes, just until firm; do not overcook. You need to have:

8 c. diced potatoes	1/2 c. chopped onion
1 lb. Velveeta cheese	Salt & pepper
1 c. Hellmann's mayonnaise	

MIX all ingredients together and place in a 9x13-inch greased baking dish.

TOP with cooked, chopped bacon and 1/4 cup sliced, stuffed olives.

BAKE 1 hour at 325°; be sure to keep covered while baking.

YIELD: 10 to 12 servings.

Side Dishes

Potatoes O'Brien

1/2 c. chopped onion	3 T. cooking oil
1/2 c. chopped green	1/4 c. beef broth
pepper	1/2 tsp. Worcestershire
1/2 c. chopped sweet	sauce
red pepper	1 tsp. salt
4 med. potatoes, cubed	

IN a skillet over medium heat, sauté the onion, pepper and potatoes in oil for 4 minutes.

COMBINE broth, Worcestershire sauce and salt; pour over vegetables.

COVER and cook for 10 minutes, or until potatoes are tender, stirring occasionally.

UNCOVER and cook until liquid is absorbed, about 3 minutes.

YIELD: 4 servings.

Scalloped Carrots

4 c. sliced carrots	1 c. diced Cheddar
1 med. onion	cheese
3 T. butter	Pepper
1 can cream of celery	2 c. herb-flavored
soup	croutons

COOK carrots until tender-crisp.

SAUTÉ onion in butter; add soup, pepper and cheese.

HEAT until cheese melts.

ADD carrots; pour into baking dish.

BAKE at 350° until bubbly, about 30 minutes.

YIELD: 6 to 8 servings.

Sour Cream-Cream Cheese Mashed Potatoes

BOIL and mash 2 to 3 pounds of red or Idaho potatoes.

4 c. mashed potatoes	1/4 tsp. garlic powder
1 c. sour cream	1/4 c. dry bread crumbs
1 (8 oz.) pkg. cream	1 tsp. butter
cheese	1/2 c. Cheddar cheese,
1 tsp. dried chives	shredded

COMBINE potatoes, sour cream, cream cheese, chives and garlic powder. Put in a greased 2-quart casserole.
COMBINE bread crumbs with butter. Sprinkle on potatoes.
BAKE at 350° for 50 to 60 minutes.
TOP with cheese and serve immediately.
YIELD: 10 to 12 servings.

NOTE: This dish can be put together a day ahead and baked just before serving.

Stuffed Shells

2 T. vegetable oil
1/2 c. chopped onions
1 T. chopped garlic
2 cans tomato sauce
1/2 tsp. salt
Dash of pepper
1 tsp. sugar
1/2 tsp. crumbled basil
  leaves
1/2 tsp. crumbled
  oregano

2 (8 oz.) pkg. cream
  cheese
2 eggs
8 oz. Mozzarella cheese,
  grated
2 T. chopped parsley
Salt & pepper
1 pkg. jumbo shells
2 T. Parmesan cheese

SIMMER onions in oil 2 to 3 minutes. Add garlic; cook 1 minute.
ADD tomato sauce, salt, pepper, sugar, basil and oregano; simmer 10 minutes. Stir occasionally.
MIX cream cheese, eggs and Mozzarella cheese together until smooth. Add salt, pepper and parsley.
COOK shells; drain well.
COVER bottom of a 9x13-inch baking dish with sauce.
STUFF shells with mix; arrange in dish.
SPOON remaining sauce over the top and sprinkle with Parmesan.
COOK 20 minutes at 350°.
LET stand for 15 minutes before serving.
YIELD: 8 to 10 servings.

Sweet Potato Mix

3 c. cooked sweet potatoes	2 eggs
1 c. sugar	1 c. canned cream
	1 tsp. vanilla

PLACE in buttered 9x13-inch baking dish.

TOPPING:

1 c. light brown sugar	1/2 c. self-rising flour
1 stick margarine, softened	1 c. chopped nuts

MIX by hand.
SPRINKLE over the top of sweet potato mixture.
BAKE at 350° for 35 minutes.

Swiss Cheese and Broccoli

1 lb. broccoli, coarsely chopped	3 T. chopped onion
Salt	1 1/4 c. milk
3 T. butter or margarine	2 c. shredded Swiss cheese
2 T. flour	2 eggs, beaten

COOK broccoli 5 minutes, or until just tender; drain.
IN a medium saucepan over medium heat, melt margarine; stir in flour and 1 1/2 teaspoons salt, until smooth.
ADD onion; cook 1 minute. Slowly stir in milk. Cook, stirring constantly, until mixture thickens.
REMOVE from heat; stir in cheese and broccoli until cheese melts lightly. Stir in beaten eggs; pour into a greased 9x13-inch pan.
BAKE 30 minutes at 325°.
YIELD: 8 servings.

Vegetable Casserole

2 cans, or 1 bag, mixed
   vegetables (if frozen,
   they must be cooked
   first in boiling water
   for 5 to 7 minutes

1 stick margarine,
   melted
1 (8 oz.) jar Cheez Whiz
1 stack Ritz crackers

MIX vegetables and 3/4 of melted margarine with Cheez Whiz. Place in buttered 9x13-inch baking dish.

CRUSH crackers and mix with remaining 1/4 of melted margarine; put on top of vegetables.

BAKE at 350° for 40 minutes.

YIELD: 6 to 8 servings.

MEAT DISHES

List Your Favorite Recipes

Recipes   **Page**

_____   _____

_____   _____

_____   _____

_____   _____

_____   _____

_____   _____

_____   _____

_____   _____

_____   _____

_____   _____

_____   _____

_____   _____

_____   _____

_____   _____

_____   _____

_____   _____

Baked Enchiladas

1 lb. ground beef	1 (16 oz.) can stewed
1 lg. onion, chopped	tomatoes, undrained
1 1/2 T. all-purpose flour	12 corn tortillas
1 T. chili powder	1/4 c. vegetable oil
1 T. garlic powder	1 med. onion, chopped
3/4 tsp. salt	1/2 c. sliced ripe olives
1/4 tsp. ground cumin	Enchilada sauce
1/4 tsp. ground sage	2 c. (8 oz.) shredded
	Monterey Jack cheese

COOK ground beef and large onion in a large skillet until meat is browned, stirring to crumble meat; drain.

ADD flour and seasonings; cook 1 minute, stirring constantly.

GRADUALLY stir in tomatoes; cook until thoroughly heated.

FRY tortillas, 1 at a time, in hot oil for 3 to 5 seconds on each side or just until softened, add more oil, if necessary.

DRAIN tortillas on paper towels.

COMBINE medium onion and olives; sprinkle over tortillas.

SPOON about 2 tablespoons meat filling on each tortilla; roll tightly and place in a 9x13x2-inch baking dish.

POUR enchilada sauce over tortillas; bake at 350° for 15 minutes.

SPRINKLE with cheese; bake an additional 5 minutes.

YIELD: 6 servings.

ENCHILADA SAUCE:

1 (10 1/2 oz.) can beef	8 cloves garlic, pressed
consommé, undiluted	2 (8 oz.) cans tomato sauce
1/2 c. butter or margarine,	2 T. chili powder
melted	2 tsp. rubbed sage
1/2 c. all-purpose flour	1 tsp. cumin

POUR consommé into measuring cup; add enough water to measure 2 cups.

COMBINE consommé and remaining ingredients in a medium saucepan, stirring until smooth.

COOK over medium heat, stirring constantly, until smooth and thickened.

YIELD: 4 cups.

Beef Dishes　　　　　　　　　　　　　　　　　　　　111

Barbecued Meat Balls

1 1/2 lb. lean ground beef   1 c. cracker crumbs
3/4 c. milk

SAUCE:
1 c. ketchup   3 T. Worcestershire sauce
2 T. vinegar   2 T. brown sugar

FORM mixture into 24 meat balls; place in greased 9x13-inch pan.
POUR sauce over meat balls and bake at 325° for 1 hour.

Basic Meat Loaf

2 lb. ground beef   1 med. onion, chopped
3/4 tsp. salt   2 eggs
1/2 tsp. pepper   1 1/2 c. crushed saltines
2 tsp. dried parsley flakes

COMBINE ground beef and the next 6 ingredients; mix well.
SHAPE meat mixture into a loaf.
PLACE on rack of lightly-greased broiler pan.
COVER top of loaf with prepared ketchup.
BAKE at 350° for 1 hour and 20 minutes.
BASTE loaf lightly with sauce that has formed.
BAKE 5 more minutes.
YIELD: 6 to 8 servings.

Bean and Beef Pie

1 lb. ground beef
2 to 3 garlic cloves, minced
1 (11 1/2 oz.) can condensed
    bean with bacon soup,
    undiluted
1 (16 oz.) jar thick & chunky
    picante sauce, divided
1/4 c. cornstarch
1 T. chopped fresh parsley
1 tsp. paprika
1 tsp. salt
1/4 tsp. pepper

1 (16 oz.) can kidney
    beans, rinsed & drained
1 (15 oz.) can black beans,
    rinsed & drained
2 c. shredded Cheddar
    cheese, divided
3/4 c. sliced green olives,
    divided
Pastry for double-crust pie
    (10")
1 c. sour cream
1 (2 1/4 oz.) can sliced
    ripe olives, drained

IN a skillet, cook beef and garlic until beef is browned; drain.
IN a large bowl, combine soup, 1 cup picante sauce, cornstarch, parsley, paprika, salt and pepper; mix well.
FOLD in beans, 1 1/4 cups cheese, 1/2 cup onions and the beef mixture.
LINE pie plate with bottom pastry; fill with bean mixture.
TOP with remaining pastry; seal and flute edges. Cut slits in the top crust.
BAKE at 425° for 30 to 35 minutes or until lightly browned.
LET stand for 5 minutes before cutting.
GARNISH with sour cream, olives, and remaining picante sauce, cheese and onions.
YIELD: 8 servings.

Beef Casserole

3 T. all-purpose flour
1 tsp. salt
1/2 tsp. pepper
2 lb. boneless round steak,
    cut into 1/2" cubes
2 T. cooking oil
1 c. water
1/2 c. beef broth
1 garlic clove, minced
1 T. dried minced onion
1/2 tsp. dried thyme
1/4 tsp. dried rosemary,
    crushed
2 c. sliced fresh mushrooms
2 c. frozen peas, thawed
3 c. mashed potatoes,
    mashed with milk &
    butter
1 T. butter or margarine,
    melted
Paprika

IN large resealable plastic bag, combine flour, salt and pepper; add beef cubes and shake to coat.

IN a skillet over medium heat, brown beef in oil.

PLACE beef and drippings in a greased, shallow 2 1/2-quart baking dish.

TO skillet, add water, broth, garlic, onion, thyme and rosemary; bring to a boil.

SIMMER, uncovered, for 5 minutes; stir in mushrooms.

POUR over meat; mix well.

COVER and bake at 350° for 1 1/2 to 1 3/4 hours or until beef is tender.

SPRINKLE peas over meat. Spread potatoes evenly over top.

BRUSH with butter; sprinkle with parsley and paprika.

BAKE 15 to 20 minutes more.

YIELD: 6 to 8 servings.

Beef Rouladen

1/4 c. Dijon mustard
8 slices top round steak,
    1/4" thick (about 2 lb.)
Salt & pepper, to taste
8 bacon strips

1 lg. onion, cut into thin
    wedges
3 T. cooking oil
3 c. beef broth
1/3 c. all-purpose flour
1/2 c. water

LIGHTLY spread mustard on each slice of steak; sprinkle with salt and pepper. Place 1 bacon strip and a few onion wedges on each slice; roll up and secure with wooden picks. Brown in a skillet in oil; drain.
ADD broth; bring to a boil.
REDUCE heat; cover and simmer for 1 1/2 hours or until meat is tender.
REMOVE meat and keep warm.
COMBINE flour and water until smooth; stir into broth. Bring to a boil, stirring constantly, until thickened and bubbly.
REMOVE wooden picks from meat and return to gravy; heat through.
YIELD: 8 servings.

Cabbage Rolls

1 1/2 lb. ground beef	1 can tomato sauce
1 1/2 lb. ground pork	Salt & pepper, to taste
5 c. cooked long-grain rice	1 c. hot water
2 med. onions, browned	3 heads cabbage, sm. to med.

CORE and steam cabbage, cut off leaves, trim stem from each leaf and dry.

MIX above ingredients well.

SCOOP meat mixture onto leaves, roll and press the ends inside. Roll, using all meat mixture.

LINE 9x13-inch pan with leftover leaves; add cabbage rolls. Cover with more leaves.

POUR in a 32-ounce can tomato sauce spiced with salt, pepper and raw chopped onion.

BAKE at 350° for 2 hours.

YIELD: 6 to 8 servings.

Cheese 'n Pasta in a Pot

2 lb. hamburger	1 (3 oz.) can mushrooms, drained
2 onions, chopped	
Dash of garlic salt	1 pt. (16 oz.) sour cream
1 (15 oz.) can Prego spaghetti sauce	1 lb. grated Mozzarella cheese
1 (16 oz.) can stewed tomatoes	1 (8 oz.) pkg. macaroni shells, cooked & drained

COOK hamburger and add onions, garlic salt, spaghetti sauce, tomatoes and mushrooms.

LAYER in a large greased casserole half the macaroni, half the hamburger mix, half the sour cream and half the cheese.

REPEAT second layer.

COVER and bake at 350° for 50 to 60 minutes.

REMOVE cover and bake 5 more minutes.

YIELD: 8 to 10 servings.

Beef Dishes

Country-Fried Steak

1 to 1 1/2 lb. boneless round
   steak
1/3 c. all-purpose flour
1/4 tsp. salt
1/4 tsp. pepper
3 T. vegetable oil
2 sm. onions, sliced

1 c. water
1/4 c. all-purpose flour
3/4 c. milk
1/4 c. brewed coffee
2 tsp. Worcestershire sauce
1/4 tsp. salt
1/4 tsp. pepper

TRIM excess fat from steak; pound steak to 1/4-inch thickness, using a meat mallet. Cut into serving-size pieces.

COMBINE 1/3 cup flour, 1/4 teaspoon salt and 1/4 teaspoon pepper. Dredge steak in flour mixture; lightly pound floured steak.

COOK steak in hot oil in skillet until browned, turning steak once. Add sliced onion and water; cover, reduce heat and simmer 30 minutes or until tender.

REMOVE steak, reserving drippings in skillet.

ADD 1/4 cup flour to drippings in skillet, stirring until smooth. Cook until browned, stirring constantly.

GRADUALLY add milk and coffee; cook over medium heat, stirring constantly, until thickened. Stir in last 3 ingredients.

SERVE steak with gravy.

YIELD: 4 to 6 servings.

Cracked-Pepper Steak

2 (8 to 12 oz.) rib-eye steaks,
   1 1/2" thick
1/4 tsp. garlic powder
Salt
1/4 c. chopped green onion

1/4 c. butter or margarine,
   melted
1 tsp. cracked black pepper,
   divided

SPRINKLE both sides of steak with garlic powder and salt; set aside.
SAUTÉ green onions in butter in a large skillet until crisp-tender.
Remove onions; set aside.
SPRINKLE 1/2 teaspoon pepper in the skillet; add steaks and cook over medium heat 8 minutes.
SPRINKLE remaining 1/2 teaspoon pepper over top of steaks; turn and continue cooking 8 minutes, or until steaks reach desired degree of doneness.
REMOVE steaks to serving platter and sprinkle with onions.
YIELD: 2 servings.

Onion-Smothered Steak

1/4 c. flour
1/8 tsp. pepper
3 med. sliced onions
1 T. vinegar
1/4 tsp. thyme
1 tsp. salt

2 T. oil
1 c. water
1 bay leaf
1 1/2 lb. round steak, cut
   3/4" thick

COMBINE flour, salt and pepper; dredge steak pieces through flour mixture and brown in 2 tablespoons oil.
ADD remaining ingredients and bake in oven at 350° for 40 to 60 minutes, until tender.

Beef Dishes

Oven Pot Roast

1 (3 to 4 lb.) chuck or
    rump roast
All-purpose flour
Pepper
1/4 c. butter or margarine,
    melted

1/2 env. dry onion soup mix
1 (10 3/4 oz.) can cream of
    mushroom soup, undiluted
1/2 c. dry white wine
1 (4 to 5 oz.) jar whole
    mushrooms, drained

ROLL roast in flour and pepper.
BROWN roast in butter in a heavy skillet; place roast in 4-quart casserole dish with lid.
COMBINE soup mix, mushroom soup and white wine; pour over roast.
COVER and bake at 325° for 2 1/2 hours.
POUR mushrooms over roast and bake an additional 30 minutes.
YIELD: 6 to 8 servings.

Oven Swiss Steak

8 bacon strips
2 c. sliced fresh mushrooms
1/2 c. chopped onion
2 T. cornstarch
1 c. whipping cream

2 lb. round steak (3/4" thick)
1 (14 1/2 oz.) can diced
    tomatoes, undrained
1 to 2 tsp. dried tarragon
2 T. water

IN a large ovenproof skillet, cook bacon until crisp. Remove, crumble and set aside. Discard all but 1/4 cup drippings.
TRIM beef; cut into serving-size pieces. Brown on both sides in drippings. Top meat with mushrooms, tomatoes and onion. Sprinkle with tarragon and bacon. Cover and bake at 325° for 1 1/4 to 1 3/4 hours or until meat is tender, basting twice.
REMOVE meat to platter. Combine cornstarch and water; add to skillet and bring to a boil. Cook and stir 2 minutes. Reduce heat. Stir in cream; simmer 3 to 4 minutes. Serve over meat.
YIELD: 6 to 8 servings.

Parmesan-Stuffing Beef Steak

1 (32 oz.) jar spaghetti
    sauce
1 tsp. dried basil
1/8 tsp. garlic powder
2 (1 lb.) top round steaks,
    1/2" thick
1/2 tsp. pepper
1 c. (4 oz.) shredded
    Mozzarella cheese
2 eggs

1 T. milk
1/2 c. herb-seasoned stuffing
    mix
1/2 c. grated Parmesan
    cheese
1/3 c. all-purpose flour
2 T. vegetable oil
1/4 c. grated Parmesan
    cheese
Hot cooked noodles

COMBINE spaghetti sauce, basil and garlic powder in a saucepan. Bring mixture to a boil, reduce heat and simmer 15 to 20 minutes; set aside.

TRIM excess fat from steaks.

SPRINKLE steaks with pepper and pound to 1/8-inch thickness, using a meat mallet. Cut each steak into 4 pieces.

PLACE about 1/4 cup Mozzarella cheese in center of 4 steak pieces. Top with remaining steak pieces; secure with wooden picks.

COMBINE eggs and milk; beat well.

COMBINE stuffing mix and 1/2 cup Parmesan cheese.

DREDGE steaks in flour and dip in egg mixture; dredge in stuffing mixture.

BROWN steak in hot oil.

REMOVE to lightly-greased, shallow, 2-quart casserole; top with sauce and sprinkle with 1/4 cup Parmesan cheese.

COVER and bake at 350° for 1 hour.

TO serve, cut each steak in half; serve over noodles.

YIELD: 8 servings.

Beef Dishes

Pot Roast - Texas-Style

1 boneless beef chuck roast (3 to 3 1/2 lb.)
2 T. cooking oil
1 (14 1/2 oz.) can tomatoes with liquid, cut up
1 (4 oz.) can chopped green chilies
2 T. taco seasoning mix
2 tsp. beef bouillon granules
1 tsp. sugar
1/4 c. cold water
3 T. all-purpose flour

IN Dutch oven, brown roast in oil.

COMBINE tomatoes, chilies, taco seasoning, bouillon and sugar; pour over the roast.

COVER and simmer 2 to 2 1/2 hours or until meat is tender.

REMOVE roast to a platter and keep warm.

FOR gravy, pour 2 cups pan juice into a saucepan.

COMBINE the cold water and flour; stir until smooth. Add to juices; cook and stir over high heat until thickened and bubbly, about 3 minutes.

SLICE roast. Serve with gravy.

YIELD: 6 to 8 servings.

Prime Rib

1 (8 lb.) roast
2 T. Worcestershire sauce
1 1/2 T. salt
1 tsp. pepper

1/2 tsp. white pepper
1 1/2 tsp. garlic powder
1 1/2 tsp. thyme, crushed

LET roast stand at room temperature for 1 hour; poke holes at 1-inch intervals with a fork.

RUB top and sides with Worcestershire sauce.

MIX all seasonings together and rub all over top and sides.

PLACE fat-side up in a roasting pan. Let stand at room temperature for 2 hours.

ROAST at 350° for 2 hours (120° for rare, 130° to 140° for medium).

REMOVE to platter and let stand 30 to 40 minutes, until internal temperature reaches 140°.

AUJUS:
1/2 c. celery
1/2 c. onion
1/2 c. carrots

3/4 c. red wine
3 c. beef broth
2 sm. cloves, chopped fine
1/2 tsp. thyme

POUR off all but 1 tablespoon drippings; add celery, onions and carrots.

COOK over medium heat 5 minutes.

ADD wine; bring to simmer for 10 minutes.

ADD broth, garlic and thyme.

BRING to a boil and simmer 10 minutes.

Beef Dishes

Seven-Layer Supper

2 c. sliced raw potatoes
2 c. chopped celery
2 c. raw hamburger
1 c. sliced raw onion
1 c. chopped green pepper

2 c. canned tomatoes
1 can cream of chicken or
    cream of mushroom soup
2 tsp. salt
1/2 tsp. pepper

PLACE ingredients in layers, in the same order as listed, in a greased baking dish.
BAKE at 350° for about 2 hours.
YIELD: 4 to 5 servings.

IF recipe is doubled, increase baking time to 3 hours. Top with shredded cheese and return to oven for an additional 3 minutes or until cheese is melted, if desired.

Spaghetti Pie

6 oz. spaghetti
2 T. butter or margarine
1/3 c. grated Parmesan
   cheese
2 eggs, well beaten
1 c. cottage cheese
1 lb. ground beef
1/2 c. chopped onions

1/4 c. chopped green pepper
1 (8 oz.) can tomatoes, diced
1 (6 oz.) can tomato paste
1 T. sugar
1 tsp. ground oregano
1/2 tsp. garlic salt
1/2 c. shredded Mozzarella
   cheese

COOK spaghetti according to package directions; drain (should be about 3 cups spaghetti).

STIR butter into hot spaghetti.

STIR in Parmesan cheese and eggs. Form spaghetti mixture into a "crust" in a buttered 10-inch pie plate. Spread cottage cheese over bottom of spaghetti crust.

IN skillet, cook ground beef, onion and green pepper until vegetables are tender and meat is browned.

DRAIN off excess fat.

STIR in undrained tomatoes, tomato paste, sugar, oregano and garlic salt; heat through.

TURN meat mixture into spaghetti crust.

BAKE, uncovered, in 350° oven for 20 minutes.

SPRINKLE the Mozzarella cheese atop.

BAKE 5 minutes longer or until cheese melts.

YIELD: 6 servings.

Beef Dishes

Southwest Stew

2 lb. beef stew meat,
   in 1" cubes
1 1/4 c. onion, chopped
2 garlic cloves, minced
2 tsp. beef bouillon granules
1/2 tsp. salt (opt.)
1 (14 1/2 oz.) can diced
   tomatoes, undrained
1 1/2 c. frozen corn
1 (4 oz.) can chopped green
   chilies

2 T. cooking oil
2 c. water
1 c. salsa
1 T. parsley flakes
1 tsp. ground cumin
3 med. carrots, diced
1 1/2 c. frozen, cut green
   beans
Hot pepper sauce (opt.)

IN a 4-quart Dutch oven over medium heat, brown meat in oil; drain.
Add the next 8 ingredients; bring to a boil.
REDUCE heat and simmer for 1 hour.
ADD carrots; return to a boil. Reduce heat and simmer for 20 minutes.
Add tomatoes, beans, corn and chilies; return to a boil.
REDUCE heat, cover and simmer for 15 to 20 minutes or until beef
and vegetables are tender. Season with hot pepper sauce, if desired.
SERVE over rice or mashed potatoes.
YIELD: 8 servings.

Swiss Steak with Vegetables

1 lb. boneless round steak
1/4 c. all-purpose flour
1/2 tsp. salt
1/2 tsp. pepper
2 T. vegetable oil
3 lg. carrots, sliced
1 lg. onion, sliced
2 stalks celery, sliced

2 (8 oz.) cans tomato sauce
1 c. water
1 T. butter or margarine
1 1/2 tsp. beef-flavored
   bouillon granules
2 tsp. browning sauce
   (Kitchen Bouquet)
Hot, cooked noodles or rice

TRIM excess fat from steak and cut steak into serving-size pieces.
COMBINE flour, salt and pepper; dredge steak in flour mixture and lightly pound floured steak, using a meat mallet.
BROWN steak in hot oil in a skillet; place in a shallow 2-quart casserole. Spoon vegetables over meat.
COMBINE tomato sauce, water, butter, bouillon granules and browning and seasoning sauce in skillet; cook over medium heat until bouillon granules dissolve.
POUR sauce over vegetables.
COVER casserole and bake at 350° for 1 hour and 10 minutes.
SERVE over noodles.
YIELD: 4 servings.

Apple-Stuffed Pork Chops

1 1/3 c. soft bread crumbs
4 T. butter or margarine
1 med. onion, finely chopped
1 celery rib, finely chopped
2 garlic cloves, minced
1 T. cooking oil
1 tart apple, chopped
1 egg, beaten

1 tsp. dried basil
1/2 tsp. salt
1/2 tsp. dried oregano
1/4 tsp. pepper
8 center-cut pork chops,
   1/2" thick
Chicken broth

IN a skillet, brown bread crumbs in butter until golden; remove and set aside. In the same skillet, sauté onion, celery and garlic in oil until tender. REMOVE from heat; add crumbs, apple, egg and seasonings; mix well.

LAY 1 pork chop flat; spoon a fourth of the stuffing on top of it. Top with another chop and secure with string. Repeat with remaining chops and stuffing.

STAND chops vertically but not touching in a deep roasting pan.

FILL pan with 1/4-inch chicken broth.

COVER and bake at 350° for 1 1/4 hours.

UNCOVER and bake 15 minutes longer or until chops are browned and no longer pink inside.

YIELD: 4 servings.

Barbecued Pork Chops

1/2 c. maple syrup	1 tsp. lemon juice
1/2 c. catsup	1/4 tsp. salt
1 T. Worcestershire sauce	1/8 tsp. pepper
1 T. steak sauce	Dash of ground cloves
1 T. prepared mustard	6 to 8 (3/4" to 1") pork
1 T. vinegar	chops
1 T. vegetable oil	

COMBINE the first 11 ingredients in a small saucepan. Bring to a boil; reduce heat and simmer 5 minutes.
GRILL chops over medium coals 10 minutes on each side. Baste with sauce, and grill an additional 15 to 20 minutes or to desired degree of doneness, basting frequently with sauce, and turning meat occasionally.
YIELD: 6 to 8 servings.

Barbecued Ribs

3/4 tsp. garlic powder	3 1/2 to 4 1/2 lb. pork
1 tsp. salt	spareribs
1/2 tsp. pepper	

SAUCE:	1/2 c. ketchup
1 (10 3/4 oz.) can condensed	1/4 c. cider vinegar
tomato soup, undiluted	2 T. Worcestershire sauce
1 sm. onion, chopped	2 tsp. chili powder
1 c. water	1 tsp. hot pepper sauce
1/2 c. light corn syrup	1/2 tsp. ground cinnamon

COMBINE garlic powder, salt and pepper; rub onto both sides of ribs.
Place in a single layer in a 10x15x1-inch baking pan.
BAKE at 325° for 30 to 35 minutes; drain off fat.
COMBINE sauce ingredients; pour over ribs.
BAKE 50 to 60 minutes longer, basting occasionally.
CUT into serving-size pieces.
YIELD: 6 to 8 servings.

Pork Dishes

Beans and Sausage

1 1/2 lb. bulk hot pork
    sausage
1 med. green pepper,
    chopped
1 med. onion, chopped
1 (31 oz.) can pork & beans
1 (16 oz.) can kidney beans,
    rinsed & drained

1 (15 1/2 oz.) can black-eyed
    peas, rinsed & drained
1 (15 oz.) can pinto beans,
    rinsed & drained
1 (15 oz.) can garbanzo
    beans, rinsed & drained
1 1/2 c. ketchup
3/4 c. packed brown sugar
2 tsp. ground mustard

IN a skillet over medium heat, brown sausage; drain.
ADD green pepper and onion; sauté until tender; drain.
ADD remaining ingredients; mix well.
POUR into a greased 9x13x2-inch baking dish.
COVER and bake at 325° for 1 hour.
UNCOVER and bake 20 to 30 minutes longer, or until bubbly.
YIELD: 12 to 16 servings.

Cranberry Ham Loaf

1 lb. ground, cooked ham
1 lb. ground fresh pork
2 eggs, slightly beaten
1/2 tsp. onion powder
1/4 tsp. salt
1/4 tsp. pepper
1 c. cracker crumbs

3/4 c. firmly-packed brown
    sugar
1 1/2 tsp. dry mustard
1/4 c. vinegar
1 c. whole-berry cranberry
    sauce

COMBINE the first 7 ingredients; mix well.
SHAPE mixture into a 9x5-inch loaf; place in a lightly-greased 12x8x2-inch baking dish.
COMBINE sugar, mustard and vinegar; mix well and spoon over ham loaf.
BAKE at 350° for 1 hour and 20 minutes, basting twice with remaining sugar mixture.
TOP loaf with cranberry sauce and bake an additional 10 minutes.
YIELD: 8 servings.

Glazed-Baked Ham

1 bone-in, fully-cooked ham (5 to 8 lb.)	1 T. grated orange peel
	1 tsp. dry mustard
1 1/2 c. orange juice	1/4 tsp. ground cloves
1 1/4 c. packed brown sugar	

SCORE surface of ham, making diamond shapes 1/2-inch deep.
PLACE in a large baking dish.
MIX remaining ingredients; pour over ham.
COVER and refrigerate overnight, turning ham occasionally.
RESERVING glaze, remove ham to a rack in a shallow roasting pan.
Insert meat thermometer.
BAKE, uncovered, at 325° until thermometer reads 140°, about 2 to 4 hours, brushing occasionally with glaze.
YIELD: 10 to 16 servings.

Ham Balls

1 lb. fully-cooked ham	1 tsp. Dijon mustard
1/2 c. dry bread crumbs	1/2 tsp. pepper, divided
1/4 c. finely-chopped green onions	1 to 2 T. vegetable oil
	2 T. all-purpose flour
3 T. chopped fresh dill or 3 tsp. dried dill, divided	1 c. water
	1 c. sour cream
1 egg, lightly beaten	Hot, cooked noodles

COMBINE ham, bread crumbs, onions, 1/2 of the dill, milk, egg, mustard and 1/4 teaspoon pepper; mix well.
SHAPE into 1-inch balls.
HEAT 1 tablespoon butter and 1 tablespoon oil in large skillet.
BROWN ham balls, adding remaining butter and oil as needed.
REMOVE ham balls to a serving dish; cover and keep warm.
POUR ham drippings into a saucepan; blend in flour. Gradually add water and stir until smooth.
COOK over low heat, stirring constantly until mixture thickens.
ADD sour cream and remaining dill and pepper; heat through. Do not boil.
POUR over the ham balls.
SERVE over the noodles.
YIELD: 6 servings.

Pork Dishes

Ham Steak

1/2 c. firmly-packed brown
    sugar
1/2 c. honey
1/2 tsp. dried mustard
6 whole cloves

1 (1") thick smoked, fully-
    cooked ham steak
    (about 2 lb.)
2 slices canned pineapple
4 maraschino cherries

COMBINE brown sugar, honey, mustard and cloves in a small saucepan; stir well. Bring to a boil; boil 2 minutes, stirring occasionally.
PLACE ham on rack of a shallow roasting pan; bake at 325° for 10 minutes.
ARRANGE pineapple slices and cherries on top of ham; spoon on glaze.
BAKE an additional 15 minutes, basting twice with drippings.
YIELD: 6 servings.

Roast Pork Tenderloin

2 T. butter or margarine,
    melted
1 tsp. dried, whole rosemary,
    crushed
1 tsp. dried, whole thyme

1 lg. clove garlic, minced
2 (1 to 1 1/2 lb.) pork
    tenderloins
1/3 c. orange marmalade
2 T. brandy

COMBINE the first 4 ingredients; brush tenderloins with butter mixture.
PLACE tenderloins, fat-side up, on rack in a shallow roasting pan. Insert meat thermometer into thickest part of meat, making sure it does not touch fat. Drizzle remaining butter mixture over meat.
BAKE at 375° for 15 to 20 minutes.
COMBINE marmalade and brandy; brush over roast.
BAKE an additional 15 to 20 minutes, or until meat thermometer registers 160° (20 to 30 minutes per pound).
YIELD: 6 servings.

Scalloped Potatoes and Pork Chops

6 pork chops	1/2 c. onions, chopped
1 T. margarine or butter	1 can cream of mushroom or
5 c. potatoes, sliced	cream of celery soup
6 slices American cheese	1 1/4 c. milk
1 tsp. salt	1/2 tsp. pepper

BROWN chops. Place 1/2 potatoes in greased baking dish.
TOP with cheese; add the rest of potatoes.
TOP with pork chops. Salt and pepper.
COOK onions in drippings.
ADD soup and milk; heat.
POUR over pork chops.
COVER with foil and bake at 350° for 1 hour.
REMOVE foil and continue baking for 30 minutes.
YIELD: 6 to 8 servings.

Smoky Baked Ribs

3 c. catsup	2 T. liquid smoke
1/2 c. firmly-packed brown	2 T. Worcestershire sauce
sugar	Red pepper, to taste (opt.)
1/2 c. molasses	6 lb. country-style pork ribs
1/4 c. prepared mustard	1/2 tsp. garlic salt
2 T. cider vinegar	1/4 tsp. pepper

COMBINE the first 8 ingredients; set aside.
CUT ribs into serving-size pieces; place in a large Dutch oven.
COVER ribs with water; add garlic salt and pepper. Bring water to a boil, cover and reduce heat and simmer 30 minutes. Drain well.
COVER ribs with sauce.
BAKE at 350° for 1 to 1 1/2 hours.
YIELD: 6 to 8 servings.

YOU may also grill these ribs over slow coals for 45 minutes, turning frequently. Brush ribs with sauce during last 15 minutes. Serve with remaining sauce, heated.

Pork Dishes

Baked Quail

1/3 c. all-purpose flour
1/2 tsp. salt
1/2 tsp. pepper
8 quail
1/2 lb. fresh mushrooms,
   sliced

1/2 c. butter or margarine,
   divided
1/4 c. + 1 T. all-purpose flour
2 c. canned diluted chicken
   broth
1/2 c. sherry
Hot, cooked rice

COMBINE 1/3 cup flour, salt and pepper. Dredge quail in flour mixture; set aside.

SAUTÉ mushrooms in 2 tablespoons butter in a large skillet 4 minutes. Remove mushrooms from skillet; drain and set aside.

MELT remaining 6 tablespoons butter in skillet; brown quail on both sides.

REMOVE quail to a 1 1/2-quart casserole.

ADD 1/4 cup plus 1 tablespoon flour to drippings in skillet; cook 1 minute, stirring constantly.

GRADUALLY add chicken broth and sherry; cook over medium heat, stirring constantly, until gravy is thickened.

STIR in mushrooms.

POUR mushroom gravy over quail.

COVER and bake at 350° for 1 hour.

SERVE over rice or with mashed potatoes.

YIELD: 4 servings.

Baked Turkey

2 T. sage	1 tsp. paprika
1 T. pepper	1/2 tsp. dry mustard
2 tsp. curry powder	1/4 tsp. allspice
2 tsp. garlic powder	3 to 4 bay leaves, crumbled
2 tsp. dried parsley flakes	1 turkey breast (4 to 4 1/2 lb.)
2 tsp. celery seed	2 c. chicken broth

COMBINE spices and mix well.

PLACE turkey on a rack in a roasting pan; rub with spice mixture. Add broth to pan.

BAKE at 350° for 2 to 3 hours or until thermometer reads 170°, basting every 30 minutes.

YIELD: 6 servings.

YOU may make your favorite stuffing as a side dish to serve with this, or you may bake it just to use for sandwiches.

Buttermilk Fried Chicken

3/4 c. buttermilk	1 (2 1/2 to 3 lb.) broiler-
1 tsp. salt	fryer, cut up
1/4 tsp. pepper	1 c. all-purpose flour
	1 1/2 c. vegetable oil

COMBINE buttermilk, salt and pepper; stir well. Skin chicken, if desired.

PLACE chicken in a shallow container and pour mixture over the top.

COVER and let stand 20 minutes, turning once. Remove chicken.

DREDGE chicken in flour, coating well.

COOK in hot oil (350°) until browned, turning to brown both sides.

REDUCE heat to 275°; cover and cook 25 minutes.

UNCOVER and cook an additional 5 minutes.

DRAIN on paper towels.

YIELD: 4 servings.

Poultry Dishes

Chicken Casserole

1/2 c. chopped fresh
   mushrooms
3 T. finely-chopped onion
2 garlic cloves, minced
4 T. butter or margarine,
   divided
3 T. all-purpose flour
1 1/4 c. milk
3/4 c. mayonnaise
4 c. cubed, cooked chicken

3 c. cooked long-grain rice
1 c. chopped celery
1 c. frozen peas, thawed
1 (2 oz.) jar diced pimento,
   drained
2 tsp. lemon juice
1 tsp. salt
1/2 tsp. pepper
3/4 c. coarsely-crushed
   corn flakes

IN a saucepan over medium heat, sauté mushrooms, onion and garlic in 3 tablespoons butter until tender. Stir in flour until gradually combined.

GRADUALLY add milk; bring to a boil.

COOK and stir for 2 minutes or until thickened and bubbly.

REMOVE from the heat; stir in mayonnaise until smooth.

ADD chicken, rice, celery, peas, pimento, lemon juice, salt and pepper; mix well.

SPOON into an ungreased 9x13x2-inch baking dish.

MELT remaining butter; toss with corn flakes.

SPRINKLE over casserole.

BAKE, uncovered, at 350° for 30 to 35 minutes or until bubbly.

YIELD: 8 to 10 servings.

Dijon Chicken Breasts

1 T. Dijon mustard
4 chicken breast halves,
   skinned
1/4 tsp. freshly-ground black
   pepper

1/3 c. butter or margarine
2 tsp. lemon juice
1/2 tsp. garlic salt
1 tsp. dried whole tarragon

SPREAD mustard on both sides of chicken and sprinkle with pepper. Cover and refrigerate for 2 to 4 hours.
MELT butter; stir in lemon juice, garlic salt and tarragon.
PLACE chicken on grill over medium coals; baste with butter sauce.
COVER and grill 20 minutes. Remove cover and grill 30 to 35 minutes or until done, turning and basting every 10 minutes.
YIELD: 4 servings.

YOU may bake this chicken in the oven; cover and bake at 350° for 20 to 25 minutes. Uncover and bake at 325° for another 25 to 30 minutes, basting every 10 minutes.

Honey-Baked Chicken

1/4 c. butter or margarine,
   melted
1/2 c. honey
1/4 c. prepared mustard
3 T. lemon juice

1 1/2 tsp. paprika
1 (2 1/2 to 3 lb.) broiler-
   fryer, cut up & skinned
1/8 tsp. salt
1/8 tsp. pepper

COMBINE butter, honey, mustard, lemon juice and paprika, stirring well.
LIGHTLY sprinkle chicken with salt and pepper; place chicken, meaty-side down, in a lightly-greased 8x12x2-inch baking dish.
POUR honey mixture over chicken; cover dish and refrigerate 3 to 4 hours.
REMOVE chicken pieces from refrigerator; bake, covered, at 325° for 30 minutes.
REMOVE cover and turn chicken pieces; bake an additional 30 minutes or until done, basting occasionally with pan drippings.
YIELD: 4 servings.

Poultry Dishes

Parmesan Chicken

1/2 c. butter or margarine
1 tsp. Worcestershire sauce
1 c. dry bread crumbs
6 to 8 boneless, skinless
   chicken breast halves

2 tsp. Dijon mustard
1/2 tsp. salt
1/2 c. grated Parmesan
   cheese

IN a pie plate or shallow bowl, combine butter, mustard, Worcestershire sauce and salt.

IN a plastic bag, combine crumbs and Parmesan cheese. Dip chicken in butter mixture, then shake in crumb mixture.

PLACE in an ungreased 9x13x2-inch baking pan.

DRIZZLE with any remaining butter mixture.

BAKE at 350° for 40 to 45 minutes, or until chicken is no longer pink and juices run clear.

YIELD: 6 to 8 servings.

Roast Chicken

1 (3 to 3 1/2 lb.) chicken,
   broiler-fryer
3 cloves garlic, halved
2 bay leaves
1/3 c. mixed fresh basil,
   oregano & thyme leaves
1/4 c. butter or margarine,
   melted
2 tsp. chopped fresh basil (opt.)

2 tsp. chopped fresh oregano
   (opt.)
2 tsp. chopped fresh thyme
   (opt.)
1/2 tsp. salt
1/4 tsp. pepper
1/4 tsp. paprika (opt.)
Additional fresh herbs, for
   garnish (opt.)

RUB skin of chicken with cut-side of 2 pieces of garlic. Place all garlic halves, bay leaves and mixed herbs in cavity of chicken. Truss chicken (you may just hook legs of the chicken together, if not comfortable with trussing).

COMBINE butter, chopped herbs, salt and pepper.

PLACE chicken, breast-side up, in a shallow roasting pan; brush chicken generously with butter mixture.

BAKE, uncovered, at 375° for 1 1/2 hours or until done, basting occasionally with remaining butter mixture during last half of baking.

REMOVE chicken to serving platter; garnish with fresh herbs.

YIELD: 4 servings.

Tarragon Chicken Casserole

2 (10 3/4 oz.) cans
   condensed cream of
   chicken soup, undiluted
2 c. half & half cream
4 tsp. dried tarragon
1/2 tsp. pepper

1 (16 oz.) pkg. linguine or
   spaghetti, cooked &
   drained
6 c. cubed, cooked chicken
1/2 c. Parmesan cheese
Paprika (opt.)

COMBINE soup, cream, tarragon and pepper in a large bowl.
STIR in the linguine and chicken.
TRANSFER to an ungreased 4-quart baking dish.
SPRINKLE with the Parmesan cheese and paprika, if desired.
BAKE, uncovered, at 350° for 30 minutes or until heated through.
YIELD: 12 servings.

Poultry Dishes

Baked Fish

1/4 c. butter or margarine, melted	Salt & pepper
2 T. lemon or lime juice	1/4 c. chopped fresh parsley, basil or oregano
2 lb. fish fillets	1 lemon or lime, thinly sliced

COMBINE butter and lemon juice; dip each fish fillet in butter mixture and arrange in a 9x13x2-inch baking dish.

SPRINKLE fillets with salt, pepper and parsley. Arrange lemon slices over fillets.

BAKE at 350° for 30 minutes, or until fish flakes easily when tested with a fork.

YIELD: about 6 servings.

Broiled Scallops

1 3/4 c. vegetable oil	1 tsp. salt
1/4 c. catsup	1 tsp. paprika
1 sm. clove garlic, minced	2 lb. fresh sea scallops

COMBINE the first 5 ingredients in a large shallow dish; stir well. Add scallops and refrigerate at least 2 hours.

REMOVE scallops from marinade; place in a 10x15x1-inch jellyroll pan.

POUR enough marinade over scallops to coat but not cover (about 1 cup).

BROIL 2 minutes; turn scallops over and broil 2 minutes or until done.

SERVE hot.

YIELD: 4 servings.

Crab-Spaghetti

1 lb. spaghetti	1 can crabmeat
1/2 c. butter	1/2 c. beer
1 sm. onion, chopped	1/2 tsp. pepper

COOK spaghetti. Melt butter and onion in a skillet; cook until onion is soft and golden. Add beer.

ADD pepper and crabmeat; stir to blend, and heat gently until crabmeat is piping hot. Stir in parsley and salt; cook 1 minute more. Pour over spaghetti. Serve.

YIELD: 6 servings.

Crispy Fried Catfish

6 med. catfish, cleaned & dressed
1 tsp. salt
1/2 tsp. pepper

1 (2 oz.) btl. hot sauce (opt.)
2 c. self-rising cornmeal
Vegetable oil
Lemon slices (opt.)

SPRINKLE catfish with salt and pepper; place in a shallow dish. Add hot sauce; marinate 1 to 2 hours in refrigerator.
PLACE cornmeal in a plastic bag; drop in catfish, 1 at a time, and shake until completely coated.
FRY in deep hot oil (375°), until fish float to the top and are golden brown.
DRAIN well.
GARNISH with lemon slices, if desired.
YIELD: 6 servings.

Honey Walleye

1 egg
2 tsp. honey
2 c. crushed butter-flavored crackers (about 45 to 50)
1/2 tsp. salt

4 to 6 walleye fillets (1 1/2 to 2 lb.)
1/3 to 1/2 c. cooking oil
Lemon wedges (opt.)

BEAT eggs; add honey.
IN plastic bag, combine crackers and salt.
DIP fish in egg mixture, then shake in bag until coated.
COOK, in a skillet in oil for 3 to 5 minutes per side, or until golden and fish flakes easily with a fork.
SERVE with lemon wedges, if desired.
YIELD: 4 to 6 servings.

Seafood Dishes

Salmon Fritters

1 1/4 c. sifted flour
1 1/2 tsp. baking powder
1 tsp. salt
1/4 c. yellow cornmeal

1 egg, slightly beaten
3/4 c. milk
1 can salmon, drained

SIFT together flour, baking powder and salt. Stir in cornmeal.
COMBINE milk and egg.
STIR in dry ingredients only until combined.
DRAIN salmon and break into bite-sized pieces and fold into batter.
DROP into hot oil at 375°. Fry just until golden brown.
DRAIN on paper towels.
SERVE with seasoned creamed peas.

Salmon Loaf

1 (14.75 oz.) can salmon
2 c. soft bread crumbs
1/3 c. onion, finely minced
1/4 c. milk
2 eggs

2 T. parsley, minced
1 T. lemon juice
1/4 tsp. salt
1/4 tsp. dill weed
Dash of pepper

DRAIN salmon, reserving 2 tablespoons liquid.
COMBINE all ingredients.
FOR loaf, place mixture in a well-greased 8 1/2 x 4 1/2 x 2 1/2-inch
loaf pan.
BAKE at 350° for 45 minutes.
YIELD: 4 to 6 servings.

Salmon Patties

1 (15 to 16 oz.) can salmon	1 1/2 tsp. baking powder
1 egg	1 1/2 c. oil
1/2 c. flour	

DRAIN salmon and set aside 2 tablespoons of the juice.
MIX salmon and egg until sticky.
STIR in salmon mixture.
FORM into patties and fry until golden brown.
SERVE with tartar sauce or Caesar salad dressing.
YIELD: 4 to 6 patties.

Shrimp Scampi

2 lb. unpeeled, med.-size fresh shrimp	3/4 c. butter or margarine, melted
1/4 c. chopped green onion	1/4 c. dry white wine
1/4 c. chopped fresh parsley	2 T. lemon juice
4 cloves garlic, crushed	3/4 tsp. salt
	1/4 tsp. ground pepper

PEEL and devein shrimp.
SAUTÉ green onions, parsley and garlic in butter until onions are tender.
REDUCE heat to low; add shrimp.
COOK, stirring frequently, 3 to 5 minutes.
REMOVE shrimp with slotted spoon to a serving dish; keep warm.
ADD remaining ingredients to butter mixture; simmer 2 minutes.
POUR butter mixture over shrimp.
YIELD: 4 servings.

DESSERTS AND DRINKS

List Your Favorite Recipes

Recipes   **Page**

Apple Cake

This delicious recipe is from Marion Eisele of Olathe, Kansas. We made both of her recipes, and they were as delicious as promised.

1/2 c. shortening	1/2 tsp. cinnamon
1 c. sugar	3 c. apples, peeled & diced
3 egg yolks	3 egg whites
3/4 tsp. baking soda	1 c. brown sugar
1/2 tsp. nutmeg	1/2 c. coconut
1 1/2 c. flour	1/2 c. chopped nuts
1/2 tsp. salt	

COMBINE shortening and sugar; add egg yolks and mix well.
SIFT dry ingredients together, and add to creamed mixture.
ADD apples and mix; spread mixture into a greased 9x13-inch baking pan.
BEAT egg whites until stiff. Add brown sugar, nuts and coconut to egg whites; spread over top of cake.
BAKE at 350° for 45 minutes.

Apple Crisp

4 c. apples	1/4 tsp. baking soda
1 c. sugar	1/4 tsp. baking powder
2 T. flour	1 c. oatmeal
1/4 tsp. cinnamon	1 c. flour
1 stick margarine, melted	1 c. brown sugar

MIX apples, sugar, flour and cinnamon together.
POUR into a greased 9x9-inch baking pan.
MIX together margarine, baking soda, baking powder, oatmeal, flour and brown sugar.
POUR over apples.
BAKE at 350° for 40 to 45 minutes.

Applesauce Cake

1/2 c. margarine	3/4 tsp. cinnamon
1 c. sugar	1 tsp. baking soda
1 egg	1 tsp. baking powder
1 1/2 c. applesauce	1 c. raisins
1/2 tsp. nutmeg	1 c. nuts
1/2 tsp. cloves	2 c. flour

CREAM together margarine and sugar; add egg and applesauce. Mix well. Sift together the nutmeg, cloves, cinnamon, baking soda, baking powder and flour.

STIR into creamed mixture and stir in nuts.

BAKE at 350° for about 45 minutes. Top with Brown Sugar Frosting.

BROWN SUGAR FROSTING:

2/3 c. brown sugar	1/2 c. coconut
3 T. cream	1/4 c. melted margarine

MIX and spread over hot cake. Brown under broiler (watch, as it browns fast).

Apricot-Almond Bread Pudding

3 c. whole wheat bread	4 eggs
(day-old, cubed)	2 c. nonfat milk
3/4 c. dried apricot halves	1/2 c. sugar
1/4 c. almonds, chopped	1/2 tsp. vanilla
& toasted	1/2 tsp. almond extract

IN a greased, shallow 1 1/2-quart casserole, lightly toss together bread cubes, apricots and almonds.

BEAT together eggs, milk, sugar and flavorings; pour over bread mixture.

COVER and refrigerate several hours or overnight.

BAKE in a preheated 350° oven until knife inserted near center comes out clean, for 45 to 55 minutes.

SERVE hot, or refrigerate to serve chilled.

YIELD: 8 servings

CARAMEL SAUCE FOR BREAD PUDDING:

1 c. cold water	1 tsp. cinnamon
1 T. cornstarch	3 T. butter
1/2 c. sugar	2 tsp. vanilla extract

COMBINE cornstarch, sugar, and cinnamon. Combine with water. Stir until dissolved.

MICROWAVE on HIGH POWER for 2 to 3 minutes, until thickened, or heat in saucepan on stove until thick and clear. Remove, add butter and vanilla.

STIR until butter is melted.

SERVE over bread pudding.

Banana Split Pie

Chocolate graham cracker
   pie crust
Crushed pineapple,
   in juice
Instant vanilla pudding

Cool Whip
2 bananas
Chocolate syrup
Strawberries, sliced

DRAIN pineapple into a bowl. Slice the bananas into the pineapple juice. Drain the bananas and put them into the pie crust.

COVER the bananas with the crushed pineapple.

MIX the vanilla pudding according to directions and pour over the pineapple.

ARRANGE the strawberries over the pudding, then cover with the Cool Whip.

DRIZZLE the chocolate syrup on top; refrigerate.

YIELD: 6 servings.

Desserts

Cherry Cream Torte

2 (3 oz.) pkg. ladyfingers
2 T. white grape or apple
  juice
1 (8 oz.) pkg. cream cheese,
  softened
2/3 c. sugar
1 tsp. almond extract, divided

2 c. whipping cream, whipped
1 (21 oz.) can cherry pie
  filling
Toasted, sliced almonds &
  additional whipped cream
  (opt.)

SPLIT ladyfingers lengthwise; brush with juice. Place a layer of ladyfingers around the sides and over the bottom of a lightly-greased 9-inch springform pan.

IN a mixing bowl, beat cream cheese until smooth; add sugar and 1/2 teaspoon extract. Beat on medium for 1 minute. Fold in whipped cream. Spread half over crust.

ARRANGE remaining ladyfingers in a spoke-like fashion. Spread evenly with the remaining cream cheese mixture.

COVER and chill overnight.

COMBINE the pie filling and remaining extract; spread over the cream cheese layer.

CHILL for at least 2 hours.

TO SERVE, remove sides of pan.

GARNISH with almonds and whipped cream if desired.

YIELD: 16 to 18 servings.

Chocolate Almond Cheese Cake

1 1/4 c. graham cracker crumbs	1/4 c. sliced almonds, toasted
1 1/2 c. sugar, divided	1/4 c. butter, melted
2 (8 oz.) pkg. cream cheese, softened	1/2 c. + 2 T. baking cocoa, divided
1 c. (8 oz.) sour cream	3 eggs
1 1/2 tsp. almond extract, divided	1 c. heavy cream
	1/4 c. confectioners' sugar

COMBINE crumbs, 1/4 cup sugar, 2 tablespoons cocoa and butter; mix well. Press into the bottom of a 9-inch springform pan; chill.

IN a mixing bowl, beat the cream cheese, sour cream and remaining sugar until smooth. Add eggs, one at a time, beating well after each addition. Stir in 1 teaspoon of extract and remaining cocoa. Pour into crust.

BAKE at 350° for 45 to 50 minutes, or until the center is almost set. Cool completely, refrigerate at least 8 hours.

IN mixing bowl, whip cream until it mounds slightly. Add confectioners' sugar and remaining extract; continue whipping until soft peaks form. Spread evenly over cheesecake.

SPRINKLE with almonds.

STORE in refrigerator.

YIELD: 12 servings.

Cinnamon Toast Pudding with Caramel Sauce

8 slices white sandwich
    bread
3 T. butter or margarine,
    softened
1/4 c. sugar
2 tsp. ground cinnamon

2 1/2 c. milk
2/3 c. sugar
Pinch of salt
1 1/4 c. eggs, beaten (may
    use egg substitute)
1 T. vanilla extract

SPREAD 1 side of each bread slice evenly with butter.

COMBINE 1/4 cup sugar and cinnamon; sprinkle evenly over buttered side of bread. Place on a baking sheet.

BROIL 4 inches from heat (with electric oven door partially open), 2 minutes or until browned and bubbly. Remove from oven; cool.

CUT each toast slice into 4 triangles. Arrange triangles, sugared-side up, on bottom and around sides of a well-buttered 9-inch quiche dish, overlapping, if necessary. Set aside.

COOK milk in a saucepan over low heat until hot; remove from heat. Add 2/3 cup sugar and next 3 ingredients, stirring until sugar dissolves.

SPOON half of custard into quiche dish; let stand 5 minutes.

POUR in remaining custard; place dish in a large shallow pan. Add hot water to larger pan to depth of 3/4-inch.

BAKE at 350° for 30 to 35 minutes, or until knife inserted in center comes out clean. Serve warm with Caramel Sauce.

YIELD: 8 servings.

CARAMEL SAUCE:

1 c. sugar
1/2 c. dark corn syrup
1 T. butter or margarine

Pinch of salt
1/4 c. evaporated milk
1 1/2 tsp. vanilla extract

COMBINE first 4 ingredients in a heavy saucepan; bring to a boil over medium heat, stirring constantly. Boil, stirring constantly, 1 minute. Remove from heat.

STIR in evaporated milk and vanilla.

YIELD: 1 1/2 cups.

Desserts

Cocoa-Almond Biscotti

1/2 c. butter or margarine,
   softened
1 c. sugar
2 lg. eggs
1 1/2 T. chocolate syrup
2 1/4 c. all-purpose flour

1 1/2 tsp. baking powder
1/4 tsp. salt
1 1/2 T. cocoa
1 (6 oz.) can whole almonds
   (1 c.)

COMBINE butter and sugar in a large bowl; beat at medium speed with an electric mixer until light and fluffy. Add eggs, beating well. Mix in chocolate syrup.

COMBINE flour and next 3 ingredients; add to butter mixture, beating well. Stir in almonds.

DIVIDE dough in half; shape each portion into a 9x2-inch log on a greased baking sheet.

BAKE at 350° for 30 minutes, or until firm. Cool on baking sheet 5 minutes. Remove to wire racks to cool completely.

CUT each log diagonally into 1/2-inch-thick slices with a serrated knife, using a gentle sawing motion. Place on ungreased baking sheets.

BAKE at 350° for 5 to 7 minutes. Turn cookies over and bake 5 to 7 additional minutes. Remove to wire racks to cool.

YIELD: 2 1/2 dozen.

Chocolate Mayonnaise Cake

2 c. flour   5 to 6 T. cocoa
1 c. sugar   1/4 tsp. salt
1 1/2 tsp. baking soda

MIX these ingredients in a large bowl.
ADD:
  1 c. mayonnaise   1 tsp. vanilla
  1 c. water

BEAT well.
POUR into a 9x9-inch greased baking pan.
BAKE at 350° for 30 to 35 minutes.

SOUR CREAM CHOCOLATE FROSTING:
MELT:
  1/2 cup semi-sweet   2 T. butter
      chocolate chips
BLEND IN:
  1/4 c. sour cream   A pinch of salt
  1/2 tsp. vanilla

ADD:
  1 1/4 c. confectioners' sugar

BEAT well.

Chocolate Chip-Cinnamon Biscotti

1/3 c. butter or margarine, softened
1/2 c. firmly-packed brown sugar
1/2 c. sugar
1 T. instant coffee
2 lg. eggs
2 c. all-purpose flour
1 1/2 tsp. baking powder
1/8 tsp. salt
1/2 tsp. ground cinnamon
1 c. chopped walnuts or pecans
1 c. semi-sweet chocolate mini morsels
2 (2 oz.) sq. vanilla candy coating, melted

COMBINE first 4 ingredients in a large bowl; beat at medium speed with an electric mixer until light and fluffy. Add eggs, 1 at a time, beating until blended.

COMBINE flour and next 3 ingredients; add butter mixture, stirring until blended. Fold in nuts and chocolate morsels.

DIVIDE dough in half, and shape each dough portion into a 10x2-inch log on a lightly-greased baking sheet.

BAKE at 350° for 25 minutes, or until firm. Cool on baking sheet 5 minutes. Remove to wire racks to cool completely.

CUT each log diagonally into 1/2-inch-thick slices with a serrated knife, using gentle sawing motion, and place slices on ungreased baking sheet.

BAKE slices at 350° for 10 minutes; turn cookies over, and bake 10 additional minutes. Remove cookies to wire racks to cool completely.

DIP 1 side of each cookie into candy coating; chill until set.

YIELD: 2 1/2 dozen.

Creme de Menthe Cake

1 pkg. Betty Crocker white cake mix
1/4 c. oil
1 c. water
1/4 c. white Karo syrup
3 T. creme de menthe

MIX cake mix according to directions, using only the ingredients listed. Mix all together and put in a 9x13-inch pan.

BAKE at 350° for 25 to 30 minutes, or until done. Cool.

TOPPING: Hershey's or Smucker's fudge topping and 1 (8-ounce) container of Cool Whip, with 3 teaspoons creme de menthe.

Fresh Peach Cobbler

2 c. fresh peaches, sliced
   (you do not have
   to peel)
4 T. butter
3/4 c. sugar

1/2 c. milk
1 tsp. baking powder
1 c. flour
1/2 tsp. salt

TOPPING:
1 c. sugar
1 c. boiling water

1 T. cornstarch
1/4 tsp. salt

PLACE sliced peaches in the bottom of an 8x8-inch square pan or
large round cake pan.
COMBINE sugar and butter.
ADD remaining dry ingredients, alternately with milk.
SPREAD over fruit.

FOR TOPPING:
MIX sugar, cornstarch and salt. Sift over batter.
POUR boiling water over all.
BAKE at 325° for approximately 50 minutes.
SERVE warm with ice cream.

German Apple Cake

1/2 c. shortening	2 tsp. cinnamon
1 c. sugar	2 tsp. baking soda
1/2 c. brown sugar	1 c. sour milk
2 eggs	2 c. raw apples, peeled &
1 1/4 c. flour	diced

BEAT shortening until smooth. Add sugars and eggs; beat until fluffy.
MIX flour and cinnamon together. Combine baking soda and sour milk. Then add the dry ingredients and the milk, alternately, to the creamed mixture.
WHEN well blended, fold in apples.
POUR into greased 9x13-inch cake pan. Sprinkle topping over cake and bake at 350° for 45 to 50 minutes.

TOPPING:

1/2 c. brown sugar	1/2 tsp. cinnamon
1/4 c. sugar	1/2 c. chopped nuts or coconut

Ginger Creams

This recipe was sent to us by Carol Moriarty Parman. It is a recipe sent by her grandmother Rosa Belle Smith Moriarty to her daughter-in-law, Marian Lisignoli (Mrs. Paul Moriarty), in 1942, before she was married to Paul.

3/4 c. shortening	1 tsp. baking soda
1 c. sugar	1/2 tsp. salt
1 egg	1 T. ginger
1/4 c. molasses	1 tsp. cinnamon
3/4 c. flour	Granulated sugar, to roll in

CREAM shortening thoroughly; add sugar and blend well.
BEAT in egg and molasses.
SIFT the dry ingredients together and add to creamed mixture.
CHILL the dough overnight in refrigerator and shape into a roll; cut and roll each in sugar.
PLACE 2 1/2 inches apart on greased cookie sheet.
BAKE in moderate oven at 375° for 12 minutes.

Desserts

Great Cherry Cake

1 devils food cake mix	1 can hot fudge sauce
1 can cherry filling	Cool Whip

PREPARE cake as directed. Poke holes in cake.
POUR 1 can hot fudge sauce over warm cake.
TOP with 1 can cherry pie filling, then top with Cool Whip.

Hot Apple-Cinnamon Sundaes

1 c. sugar	1/2 tsp. ground cinnamon
1 c. orange juice	10 c. sliced, peeled apples
1/2 c. lemon juice	1 1/2 qt. vanilla ice cream

IN a saucepan over medium heat, bring sugar, juices and cinnamon to a boil.
REDUCE heat, simmer, uncovered, for 5 minutes.
ADD apples and return to a boil.
REDUCE heat; cover and simmer 15 minutes, or until apples are tender.
SERVE warm over ice cream.
SPRINKLE with cinnamon, if desired.
YIELD: 12 servings (5 cups topping).

Mandarin Orange Cake

1 c. sugar	1 egg
1 c. flour	1 sm. can mandarin
1 tsp. baking soda	oranges, drained
1/2 tsp. salt	Chopped nuts
1 tsp. vanilla	

TOPPING:
BOIL:

3/4 c. brown sugar	3 T. milk
3 T. margarine	

COMBINE cake ingredients and beat 2 to 3 minutes.
BAKE at 350° for 30 to 35 minutes in a greased 9x9-inch pan.
PUNCH holes in top of cake and pour topping over as soon as it is out of the oven.
TOP with whipped cream or Cool Whip, if desired.

Oatmeal Cake

1 1/4 c. boiling water	1 1/2 c. flour
1 c. oatmeal	1 tsp. baking soda
1/2 c. margarine, softened	2 tsp. baking powder
1 c. brown sugar	1 tsp. cinnamon
1 c. granulated sugar	1 tsp. salt
2 eggs	

POUR boiling water over oatmeal; set aside.
CREAM together margarine, sugars and eggs. Then add oatmeal mixture and the remaining ingredients.
POUR batter into a greased 9x13-inch baking pan and bake at 350° for 30 minutes.
COOL cake and spread with topping.
PUT under broiler until topping bubbles, about 2 minutes.

TOPPING:

1/4 c. butter or margarine, softened	1/4 c. milk
	1 c. coconut
2/3 c. brown sugar	1 c. pecans, chopped

Desserts

One-Crust Peach Pie

1 egg white	1/3 c. sugar
1 unbaked pastry shell (9")	1/4 c. chilled butter or margarine, cut in pieces
3/4 c. all-purpose flour	6 c. sliced, fresh peaches
1/2 c. packed brown sugar	

BEAT egg white until foamy; brush over the bottom and sides of the pastry.

COMBINE flour and sugar in a small bowl; cut in butter until mixture resembles fine crumbs.

SPRINKLE two-thirds into the bottom of the pastry; top with peaches.

SPRINKLE with the remaining crumb mixture.

BAKE at 375° for 40 to 45 minutes, or until filling is bubbly and peaches are tender.

YIELD: 6 to 8 servings.

Peanut Butter Cream Pie

1 (8 oz.) pkg. cream cheese, softened	1 (8 oz.) ctn. frozen whipped topping, thawed
3/4 c. confectioners' sugar	1 (9") graham cracker crust
1/2 c. creamy peanut butter	1/4 c. chopped peanuts
6 T. milk	

IN A MIXing bowl, beat cream cheese until fluffy.

ADD sugar and peanut butter; mix well.

GRADUALLY add the milk.

FOLD in whipped topping; spoon into the crust.

SPRINKLE with peanuts.

CHILL overnight.

YIELD: 6 to 8 servings.

Orange-Pecan Baked Apples

6 med. baking apples,
cored
1/4 c. orange marmalade

2 T. finely-chopped pecans
Ground cinnamon
Ground nutmeg

PLACE apples in a shallow, ungreased baking pan; add a small amount of water to pan.

IN a small bowl, combine marmalade and pecans; mix well.

FILL center of apples with marmalade mixture; sprinkle with cinnamon and nutmeg.

BAKE, uncovered, at 350° for 60 to 70 minutes, or until apples are tender.

YIELD: 6 servings.

Raspberry Cheese Cake

2 c. chocolate wafer
    crumbs

1/3 c. butter or margarine,
    melted
3 T. sugar

RASPBERRY SAUCE:
2 1/2 c. fresh or frozen
    raspberries, thawed,
    unsweetened

2/3 c. sugar
2 T. cornstarch
2 tsp. lemon juice

FILLING/TOPPING:
3 (8 oz.) pkg. cream
    cheese, softened
1/2 c. sugar
2 T. all-purpose flour
1 tsp. vanilla extract
2 egg whites

1 c. whipping cream
2 to 3 T. orange juice
1 1/2 c. fresh or frozen
    unsweetened raspberries,
    thawed

COMBINE the first 3 ingredients; press into bottom and 1 1/2 inches
up sides of a greased 9-inch springform pan.
CHILL 1 hour, or until firm.
PURÉE raspberries in a blender or food processor. Press through a
sieve; discard seeds. Add water, if necessary, to measure 1 cup.
IN a saucepan, combine sugar and cornstarch. Stir in raspberry juice;
bring to a boil. Boil 2 minutes, stirring constantly.
REMOVE from heat; stir in lemon juice and set aside.
IN a mixing bowl, beat cream cheese, sugar, flour and vanilla until
fluffy. Add egg whites; beat on low just until blended. Stir in cream.
Pour half into crust. Top with 3/4 cup raspberry sauce (cover and
refrigerate remaining sauce).
CAREFULLY spoon remaining filling over sauce.
BAKE at 375° for 35 to 40 minutes, or until center is nearly set.
REMOVE from oven; immediately run a knife around pan to loosen crust.
COOL on a wire rack 1 hour.
REFRIGERATE overnight.
ADD orange juice to chilled raspberry sauce; gently fold in raspberries.
SPOON over cheesecake.
YIELD: 12 to 16 servings.

Spiced Pears

1 (16 oz.) can pear halves   3/4 tsp. ground nutmeg
1/3 c. brown sugar   3/4 tsp. ground cinnamon

DRAIN pears, reserving syrup; set aside pears.
PLACE syrup, brown sugar, nutmeg and cinnamon in a saucepan.
Bring to a boil. Reduce heat and simmer, uncovered, for 5 minutes,
stirring frequently.
ADD pears and simmer about 5 minutes more, or until heated through.
YIELD: 4 servings.

These dessert recipes were submitted by Margaret Frick. Margaret lived 19 years in Scott, Muscatine and Cedar counties, she now resides in Ankeny, IA.

Oatmeal Pie

1 c. sugar	1/4 c. dark syrup
1/4 c. butter or margarine	1/4 c. quick oatmeal
2 eggs	1/2 c. coconut
Salt	1 (8" or 9") prepared
1/2 tsp. vanilla	pie shell
1/2 c. milk	

BEAT together sugar, butter, pinch of salt, and vanilla.
ADD milk, syrup, oatmeal and coconut; put into pie shell.
BAKE at 350° for 45 minutes.

Sour Cream Apple Pie

5 lg. peeled Granny Smith	1 T. lemon juice
apples	

TOSS apples and lemon juice together.

1 1/4 c. sugar	1 tsp. cinnamon
2/3 c. flour	1/4 tsp. nutmeg
1/2 tsp. salt	1/3 c. melted butter

MIX these ingredients together.

1 c. sour cream

IN unbaked pie shell, place apples; top with crumb mixture; spread sour cream over the top.
BAKE at 350° for 50 minutes.

Apple Cinnamon Shake

1 c. plain nonfat yogurt
1/2 c. applesauce, frozen
2 T. brown sugar
1/2 tsp. ground cinnamon
1/2 tsp. vanilla extract

COMBINE all ingredients in a blender until smooth.
YIELD: 1 to 2 servings (1 1/2 cups).

Autumn Harvest Punch

2 c. water
1 1/2 to 2 c. sugar
4 (3") sticks cinnamon
36 whole cloves
2 qt. cranberry juice
   cocktail
1 qt. orange juice
1 1/2 to 2 c. lemon juice
1 lemon, sliced
1 orange, sliced
1 c. rum, or 2 T. rum
   flavoring

COMBINE first 4 ingredients in a large Dutch oven; bring to a boil over high heat. Reduce heat, and simmer 7 minutes. Remove and discard spices.
ADD cranberry juice cocktail and remaining ingredients; cook over medium heat until thoroughly heated. Serve warm.
YIELD: About 5 quarts.

Banana Smoothie

2 c. milk
2 med. ripe bananas
1/4 c. honey
1/2 tsp. vanilla extract

COMBINE all ingredients in a blender until smooth.
YIELD: 3 to 4 servings (3 1/2 cups).

Berry Mimosas

6 oz. frozen orange juice
   concentrate
6 oz. frozen pineapple
   juice concentrate
2 c. raspberry juice

1 (12 oz.) can lemon-lime
   soda, chilled
Orange slices & fresh frozen
   raspberries, for garnish

IN a pitcher or punch bowl, combine all the juices.
JUST before serving, add soda, orange slices and raspberries.
YIELD: 4 servings.

Fruit Juice Punch

3 c. pineapple juice
2 c. water
2 c. apple juice
1 (6 oz.) can frozen
   lemonade concentrate,
   undiluted

1 (6 oz.) can frozen orange
   juice concentrate,
   undiluted
2 tsp. lemon instant tea mix
2 c. ginger ale, chilled

COMBINE first 6 ingredients in a large bowl, stirring well. Cover and chill at least 2 hours.
STIR in ginger ale.
YIELD: about 2 1/2 quarts.

Fruit Slush

PROCESS 1 cup refrigerated sliced mango, 1 cup plain yogurt, 1 sliced banana and 1 tablespoon honey in a blender until smooth.
ADD enough ice to bring mixture to 3 1/2-cup level, and process until smooth.

Drinks

Hot Chocolate

3 c. milk
3/4 c. half & half
1/2 c. sugar
1/2 c. cocoa

1 tsp. vanilla extract
1/3 to 1/2 c. bourbon (opt.)
Marshmallows (opt.)

COMBINE milk and half & half in a medium saucepan; cook over medium heat until thoroughly heated (do not boil).
ADD sugar and cocoa, whisking until blended. Remove from heat; whisk in vanilla and bourbon (if used).
POUR into mugs; top with marshmallows, if desired.
YIELD: 4 1/2 cups.

Hot Cranberry Drink

2 c. fresh or frozen
   cranberries
6 c. water, divided
1 c. sugar

1/4 c. red-hot candies
7 whole cloves
1/2 c. fresh orange juice
1/4 c. lemon juice

IN a saucepan, cook cranberries in 2 cups of water until they pop. Strain through a fine sieve, reserving juice and discarding skins; set aside.
IN a large saucepan, combine sugar, candies, cloves and remaining water.
COOK until candies are dissolved. Add orange and lemon juices and reserved cranberry juice; heat through.
REMOVE cloves; serve hot.
YIELD: 6 to 8 servings (2 quarts).

Ice Cream Coffee

1 to 2 T. superfine sugar,
   or to taste
3 c. double-strength,
   freshly-brewed,
   dark roast coffee

Ice
2 scoops vanilla ice cream

STIR sugar into coffee until dissolved.
FILL 2 tall glasses with ice. Pour over ice cubes. Ice cubes will melt into coffee and dilute it to regular strength as it chills.
REMOVE unmelted ice cubes and add vanilla ice cream.
SERVE with a long-handled spoon.
YIELD: 2 servings.

Peach Slush

1 (16 oz.) can sliced
   peaches, drained
1 (6 oz.) can frozen
   orange juice
   concentrate, thawed

1 1/2 c. apricot nectar
2 c. chilled lemon-lime soda

IN a blender, combine peaches, orange juice and nectar; blend until smooth.
POUR into a freezer container; cover and freeze until firm.
TO SERVE, scoop 2/3 cup frozen mixture into a glass; add 1/3 cup soda.
YIELD: 6 servings.

Slush Fruit Cups

1 (20 oz.) can crushed
    pineapple
1 (10 oz.) pkg. frozen
    strawberries in
    juice, thawed
1 (6 oz.) can frozen
    orange juice
    concentrate, thawed

1 (6 oz.) can frozen
    lemonade concentrate,
    thawed
3 firm bananas, cut into
    1/4" slices
1 1/2 c. lemon-lime soda
1 c. water
1 c. sugar
20 paper cups (5 oz.)

IN a large bowl, mix pineapple, strawberries, orange juice, lemonade, bananas, baking soda, water and sugar. Pour about 1/2 cup into each paper cup.
COVER with foil and freeze until firm.
REMOVE from freezer 15 minutes before serving.
SERVE in a dessert cup.
YIELD: 20 servings (1/2 cup).

Tropical Refresher Slush

1 banana, cut into fourths
1 c. refrigerated sliced
    mango

1 c. fresh pineapple chunks

FREEZE these ingredients on a baking sheet for 30 minutes.
COMBINE frozen fruit in a blender until smooth, with:

1 cup milk
    (may use skim)
1 cup vanilla low-fat yogurt

2 tablespoons honey
1 teaspoon lime juice
1/2 teaspoon vanilla extract

YIELD: 4 servings.

HINTS AND HOW-TO'S

List Your Favorite Recipes

Recipes   **Page**

_____   _____

_____   _____

_____   _____

_____   _____

_____   _____

_____   _____

_____   _____

_____   _____

_____   _____

_____   _____

_____   _____

_____   _____

_____   _____

_____   _____

_____   _____

_____   _____

_____   _____

Create Your Own Casserole

You may choose any one of four different casseroles. Each casserole bakes for 1 hour and 20 minutes. You do not have to precook the pasta or rice.

CHICKEN CASSEROLE: Cream of chicken soup, broccoli, rice, chicken, Parmesan cheese, bread crumbs.

HAM CASSEROLE: Cream of celery soup, green beans, egg noodles, ham, garlic, 2 portions Swiss cheese.

TURKEY CASSEROLE: Italian-style diced tomatoes, spinach, medium pasta shells, turkey, onion, garlic, Mozzarella cheese, bread crumbs.

VEGETARIAN CASSEROLE: Italian-style diced tomatoes, yellow squash, rice, olives, 4 portions of celery, 4 portions bell pepper, garlic, Parmesan cheese, bread crumbs.

DIRECTIONS

COMBINE 1 cup sour cream, 1 cup milk, 1 cup water, 1 teaspoon salt and 1 teaspoon pepper with Sauce Maker (omit sour cream and milk when using tomatoes). Stir in Frozen Vegetable, Pasta/Rice/Meat/Fish/Poultry, and, if desired, Extras. Spoon into lightly-greased 9x13-inch baking dish; sprinkle with toppings.

BAKE casserole, covered, at 350° for 1 hour and 10 minutes; uncover and bake 10 minutes more.

YIELD: 6 servings.

CHOOSE ONE SAUCE MAKER:
1 (10 3/4 ounce) can cream of mushroom soup, undiluted.
1 (10 3/4 ounce) can cream of celery soup, undiluted.
1 (10 3/4 ounce) can cream of chicken soup, undiluted.
1 (10 3/4 ounce) can Cheddar cheese soup, undiluted.
1 (10 3/4 ounce) can Italian-style diced tomatoes, undrained.

CHOOSE ONE FROZEN VEGETABLE:
1 (10 ounce) package frozen, chopped spinach, thawed.
1 (10 ounce) package frozen cut broccoli.
1 (10 ounce) package frozen Italian green beans.
1 (10 ounce) package English peas.
1 (10 ounce) package frozen, sliced yellow squash.
1 (10 ounce) package frozen whole kernel corn.

CHOOSE ONE PASTA/RICE:
2 cups uncooked elbow macaroni.
1 cup uncooked rice.
4 cups uncooked wide egg noodles.
3 cups uncooked medium shells.

CHOOSE ONE MEAT/FISH/POULTRY:
2 (6-ounce) cans solid white tuna, drained and flaked.
2 cups chopped cooked chicken.
2 cups chopped cooked ham.
2 cups chopped cooked turkey
1 pound ground beef, browned and drained.

CHOOSE ONE OR MORE EXTRAS (OPTIONAL):
1 (3-ounce) can sliced mushrooms, drained.
1/4 cup sliced ripe olives.
1/4 cup chopped bell pepper.
1/4 cup chopped onion.
1/4 cup chopped celery.
2 cloves garlic, minced.
1 (4.5 ounce) can chopped green chilies.
1 (1 1/4 ounce) package taco seasoning mix.

CHOOSE ONE OR TWO TOPPINGS:
1/2 cup (2 ounces) shredded Mozzarella cheese.
1/2 cup grated Parmesan cheese.
1/2 cup (2 ounces) shredded Swiss cheese.
1/2 cup fine, dry bread crumbs.

Spice and Herb Guide

ALLSPICE: A pea-sized fruit that grows in Mexico, Jamaica, Central and South America. Its delicate flavor resembles a blend of cloves, cinnamon and nutmeg. USES: (whole) pickles, meats, boiled fish, graves; (ground) puddings, relishes, fruit preserves, baking.

BASIL: The dried leaves and stems of an herb grown in the United States and North Mediterranean area. Has an aromatic, leafy flavor. USES: For flavoring tomato dishes and tomato paste, turtle soup; also use in cooked peas, squash, snap beans; sprinkle chopped over lamb chops and poultry.

BAY LEAVES: The dried leaves of an evergreen grown in the eastern Mediterranean countries. Has a sweet, herbaceous floral spice note. USES: For pickling, stews, for spicing sauces and soup. Also use with a variety of meats and fish.

CARAWAY: The seed of a plant grown in the Netherlands. Flavor that combines the tastes of Anise and Dill. USES: For baking breads, often added to sauerkraut, noodles, cheese spreads. Also adds zest to French-fried potatoes, liver, canned asparagus.

CURRY POWDER: A ground blend of ginger, turmeric, fenugreek seed, as many as 16 to 20 spices. USES: For all Indian curry recipes such as lamb, chicken and rice, eggs, vegetables and curry puffs.

DILL: The small, dark seed of the dill plant grown in India, having a clean aromatic taste. USES: Dill is predominant seasoning in pickling recipes; also adds pleasing flavor to sauerkraut, potato salad, cooked macaroni and green apple pie.

MACE: The dried covering around the nutmeg seed. Its flavor is similar to nutmeg, with a fragrant, delicate difference. USES: (whole) for pickling, fish, fish sauce, stewed fruit; (ground) delicious in baked goods, pastries and doughnuts, adds unusual flavor to chocolate desserts.

MARJORAM: An herb of the mint family, grown in France and Chile. Has a minty-sweet flavor. USES: In beverages, jellies, and to flavor soups, stews, soups, chowder, chop suey and cooked vegetables.

MSG (MONOSODIUM GLUTAMATE): Is a vegetable protein derivative for raising the effectiveness of natural food flavors. USES: Small amounts, adjusted to individual taste, can be added to steaks, roasts, chops, seafood, stews, soups, chowder, chop suey and cooked vegetables.

OREGANO: A plant of the mint family and a species of marjoram of which the dried leaves are used to make an herb seasoning. USES: An excellent flavoring for any tomato dish, especially pizza, chili con carne and Italian dishes.

PAPRIKA: A mild, sweet red pepper growing in Spain, Central Europe and the United States. Slightly aromatic and prized for brilliant red color. USES: A colorful garnish for pale foods, and for seasoning Chicken Paprika, Hungarian Goulash, salad dressings.

POPPY: The seed of a flower grown in Holland. Has a rich fragrance and crunchy, nut-like flavor. USES: Excellent as a topping for breads, rolls and cookies. Also delicious in buttered noodles.

ROSEMARY: An herb (like a curved pine needle) grown in France, Spain and Portugal, and having a sweet, fresh taste. USES: In lamb dishes, in soups, stews, and to sprinkle on beef before roasting.

SAGE: The leaf of a shrub grown in Greece, Yugoslavia and Albania. Flavor is camphoraceous and minty. USES: For meat and poultry stuffing, sausages, meat loaf, hamburgers, stews and salads.

Hints and How-To's

THYME: The leaves and stems of a shrub grown in France and Spain. Has a strong, distinctive flavor. USES: For poultry seasoning, in croquettes, fricassees and fish dishes. Also tasty on fresh sliced tomatoes.

TURMERIC: A root of the ginger family, grown in India, Haiti, Jamaica and Peru, having a mild, ginger-pepper flavor. USES: As a flavoring and coloring in prepared mustard and in combination with mustard as a flavoring for meats, dressings, salads.

Kitchen Hints

If you've over-salted soup or vegetables, add cut raw potatoes and discard once they have cooked and absorbed the salt.

A teaspoon each of cider vinegar and sugar added to salty soup of vegetables will also remedy the situation.

If you've over-sweetened a dish, add salt.

A teaspoon of cider vinegar will take care of too-sweet vegetables or main dishes.

Pale gravy may be browned by adding a bit of instant coffee straight from the jar...no bitter taste.

If you will brown the flour well before adding to the liquid when making gravy, you will avoid pale or lumpy gravy.

A different way of browning flour is to put it in a custard cup placed beside meat in oven. Once the meat is done, the flour will be nice and brown.

Thin gravy can be thickened by adding a mixture of flour or cornstarch and water, which has been mixed to a smooth paste, added gradually, stirring constantly, while bringing to a boil.

Lumpless gravy can be your triumph if you add a pinch of salt to the flour before mixing it with the water.

A small amount of baking soda added to gravy will eliminate excess grease.

Drop a lettuce leaf into a pot of homemade soup to absorb excess grease from the top.

Hints and How-To's

If time allows, the best method of removing fat is refrigeration until the fat hardens. If you put a piece of waxed paper over the top of the soup, etc., it can be peeled right off, along with the hardened fat.

Ice cubes will also eliminate the fat from soups and stews. Just drop a few into the pot and stir; the fat will cling to the cubes; discard the cubes before they melt. Or, wrap ice cubes in paper towel or cheesecloth and skim over the top.

If fresh vegetables are wilted or blemished, pick off the brown edges, sprinkle with cool water, wrap in a paper towel and refrigerate for an hour or so.

Perk up soggy lettuce by adding lemon juice to a bowl of cold water and soak for an hour in the refrigerator.

Hints for Soups, Stews and Sandwiches

You can use instant potatoes instead of flour to thicken soups, stews and gravies without lumps. Another excellent thickener for soup is a little oatmeal. It will add flavor and richness to almost any soup.

If soup has been over-salted, add a teaspoon of sugar or a few pieces of raw turnip and simmer a little longer. This will neutralize the salt flavor.

Grate a raw potato and add it to your soup when it is too salty. Or add a whole, raw potato and remove before serving. The potato absorbs the salt.

All seasonings should be added gradually to soup or the flavor may be too strong.

A little finely-grated cheese added to thin soup improves the taste immensely.

Remember, soup boiled is soup spoiled. Soup should be cooked gently and evenly.

To prevent curdling of milk or cream in soup, add the soup to the milk rather than vice versa. Or add a bit of flour to the milk and beat well before combining.

Cream soups tend to boil over easily. Some cooks say that greasing the top edges of the cooking container will prevent this problem. One quart of soup yields about 6 servings, unless it is the main course.

Vegetables added to the soup will make a much tastier dish, if you sauté them first, preferably in a little butter.

A leaf of lettuce dropped into the pot absorbs the grease from the top of the soup. Remove the lettuce and throw it away as soon as it has served its purpose. Or, float a piece of tissue paper lightly on top of the soup and it will absorb the grease.

Hints and How-To's

Fat can be skimmed off soup by chilling soup until fat hardens. If time does not permit this, wrap ice in paper toweling and skim over the top.

Steak, roast or poultry bones can be frozen until needed for soup stock.

Always start cooking bones and meat in cold, salted water.

Instant soup stock will always be on hand if you save the pan juices from cooking meats. Pour the liquid into ice cube trays and freeze. Place solid cubes in freezer bags or foil.

Lettuce and celery keep longer if you store them in paper bags instead of cellophane.

To remove the core from a head of lettuce, hit the core-end once against the counter sharply. The core will loosen and pull out easily.

Cream will whip faster and better if you'll first chill the cream, bowl and beaters well.

Soupy whipped cream can be saved by adding an egg white, then chilling thoroughly. Rebeat for a fluffy surprise.

A few drops of lemon juice added to whipping cream helps it whip faster and better.

Cream whipped ahead of time will not separate if you add 1/4 teaspoon unflavored gelatin per cup of cream.

A dampened and folded dish towel placed under the bowl in which you are whipping cream will keep the bowl from dancing all over the countertop.

Brown sugar won't harden if an apple slice is placed in the container.

But if your brown sugar is already brick-hard, put your cheese-grater to work and grate the amount you need.

Hints for Breads and Spreads

Dry yeast is soaked or softened in warm liquid. Technically, you cannot "dissolve the yeast"; it is a living organism. Cells merely separate, activate and reconstitute to expand and reproduce. They will appear to dissolve only because the cells are exceedingly small.

Hot water kills yeast. You can tell if the temperature is correct by pouring the water over your forearm; if you cannot feel either hot or cold, the temperature is just right.

Add 1/2 teaspoon of sugar to the yeast when stirring it into the water to soften. If it foams and bubbles in ten minutes, you know the yeast is alive and active.

There is a difference in the yeast called for in old recipes and today's. A "cup of yeast" called for in some older recipes is similar to sourdough batter; "2 ounces" yeast called for in a 1954 cookbook is equal to a one-fourth ounce envelope of today's yeast.

Use water that has been used to boil potatoes to make bread more moist; adds flavor and provides food for the yeast.

When milk is used in making bread, you get a finer texture. Water makes a coarser bread.

When creaming butter and sugar together, it's a good idea to rinse the bowl first with boiling water. They cream faster.

Dough won't stick to your hands if kneaded inside a large plastic bag.

To help yeast dough rise quickly and evenly, using a heating pad. Set the covered bowl on the pad with its temperature set at medium. If the television is in use, it makes a nice warm spot for your dough to rise.

Another way to raise bread; turn oven to 200°. When temperature is reached, shut off oven and put bread in to rise.

Hints and How-To's

Dough can be raised in 15 minutes using a microwave. Place dough in a microwave-proof bowl and put it in the microwave with another container of 8 ounces of water. Heat at 10% power (or lowest setting) for 3 minutes. Let rest in the oven for 3 minutes, then heat again for 3 minutes. Let rise 6 minutes. Dough should have doubled in bulk and is ready for shaping.

Use shortening, not oleo, to grease pans; especially for bread, as oleo and oil are absorbed more readily into the dough and do not help release baked goods from pan.

Egg Hints

SELECTING EGGS: The U.S. Department of Agriculture lists six size categories of eggs; jumbo, extra-large, large, medium, small and peewee, although all markets do not carry each size. Size does not matter much when cooking whole eggs, but for recipes with beaten eggs in specified numbers, the size can make a big difference. You should always use large eggs when making a recipe.

Eggs are graded as AA, A and B. The higher quality grades are AA and A and are good for cooking--especially when appearance is important, such as frying or poaching, because the white part of the egg is thick and the yolk is firm. Grade B eggs are good for general cooking and baking. There is no difference in nutritional value among the grades of eggs. There is no difference in flavor, nutritional value or cooking performance in the color of eggs.

Always store eggs in the refrigerator; they will keep up to five weeks without significant loss of quality. Refrigerate hard-cooked eggs as soon after cooking as possible, and use them within a week.

If you have yolks or whites left over from recipes, you can refrigerate them for several days. Place leftover whites in an airtight container and use within 10 days. Leftover yolks are more fragile. Store them in water in a tightly covered container, and use within 2 days.

It is important to make sure your eggs are kept properly stored, and are cooked thoroughly before serving.

USES FOR LEFTOVER EGG WHITES:

Frost fresh grapes for an edible garnish by lightly dipping them in unbeaten egg white and sprinkling with granulated sugar.

When baking a pie with a juicy filling, brush the bottom and sides of the pastry shell with unbeaten egg white before adding the filling; this helps keep the pastry shell from being soggy after baking.

Give homemade yeast bread a pretty shine by lightly brushing the top of the loaf with a small amount of unbeaten egg white before putting in the oven to bake.

ORDER BLANK

NAME _____

ADDRESS _____

CITY & STATE _____ ZIP _____

How many copies? _____ Amount enclosed _____
    Price per book $12.00
    Postage & handling 2.50
    Total $14.50
Please make checks payable to:
                  The Machine Shed
Mail orders to: The Machine Shed Great Farm Fixins
                  111 W. 76th Street
                  Davenport, IA 52806

ORDER BLANK

NAME _____

ADDRESS _____

CITY & STATE _____ ZIP _____

How many copies? _____ Amount enclosed _____
    Price per book $12.00
    Postage & handling 2.50
    Total $14.50
Please make checks payable to:
                  The Machine Shed
Mail orders to: The Machine Shed Great Farm Fixins
                  111 W. 76th Street
                  Davenport, IA 52806

ORDER BLANK

NAME _____

ADDRESS _____

CITY & STATE _____ ZIP _____

How many copies? _____ Amount enclosed _____
    Price per book $12.00
    Postage & handling 2.50
    Total $14.50
Please make checks payable to:
                  The Machine Shed
Mail orders to: The Machine Shed Great Farm Fixins
                  111 W. 76th Street
                  Davenport, IA 52806